Do It Now!

Do It Now!

ഔ

By Doug Meharg

BOUND
PUBLISHING

▊BOUND
▊PUBLISHING

Copyright 2012 by Doug Meharg

This book may not be reproduced in whole or in part, by any means, without written consent of the publisher.

Bound Publishing
A division of Dean Global Group Inc.

United States
6501 E. Greenway Pkwy
#103-480
Scottsdale, AZ
85254

Canada
Suite 114
720 28th St. NE
Calgary, AB T2A 6R3

Toll Free Phone and Fax: 1-888-237-1627
Email: info@boundpublishing.com

ISBN (softcover):   978-0-9867762-8-1
ISBN (ebook):   978-0-9881235-2-6

Cover: Anamarie Seidel
Text: Doug Meharg
Edit: Bound Publishing

CONTENTS

Chapter 1:	My Story	**1**
Chapter 2:	Discovering Who You Are	**23**
Chapter 3:	Keep Your Eyes on the Prize	**33**
Chapter 4:	Success Factor#1: Overcoming Obstacles	**43**
Chapter 5:	Success Factor#2: Good Decision-Making Leads to Success	**47**
Chapter 6:	Success Factor#3: Goalsetting Helps You Get What You Want	**53**
Chapter 7:	Success Factor#4: Keeping the Faith	**59**
Chapter 8:	Success Factor#5: Seeing Success in Your Mind's Eye	**63**
Chapter 9:	Managing Your Money	**67**
Chapter 10:	Put Your Money to Work	**77**
Chapter 11:	You're Richer Than You Think	**83**
Chapter 12:	Put Your Money to Work	**89**
Workbook:		**93**

1

MY STORY

I was born in 1931, the son of an Irish-Canadian father and mother. We lived on a small truck farm north of Toronto, Ontario, Canada, where my parents grew fruit and vegetables and kept chickens and a few other animals. We sold our produce at a Farmer's Market in Toronto. There were four kids in our family: my older brother James, my twin brother Gerry, and my brother Victor.

The farmhouse was a small bungalow—a living room, two bedrooms, and a kitchen. It was straight out of *Little House on the Prairie.* There was no electricity, no indoor plumbing, no running water, and the wood/coal-burning stove in the kitchen was used both for cooking and heating. Mom cooked all our meals on that stove during the fall, winter and spring. In the summer she cooked outdoors using a stove that burned coal oil. We took our goods to market in a horse-drawn wagon.

Sitting here in my air conditioned living room with its wide screen TV, telephone, central heating, track lighting, with a brand new car in the garage, I sometimes think back and wonder how so many changes could have taken place in the span of a single lifetime. People my age have seen and had to adjust to more change than any of the generations that preceded us. However if you're a young person, I predict you'll see changes on the same scale during your lifetime. That's today's world.

Back to the 1930s. Mom and Dad often had relatives in for dinner on Sunday nights and after the dishes were done and the kids put to bed, they'd sit around and talk about family news. My twin brother Gerry and I slept in the same bed, like most siblings did in that era. Before I drifted off to sleep, I would listen in on the conversation. They'd say that Gerry was a smart kid but he was not very strong. He was often sick and lacked my stamina. On the other hand, I would hear them say I was strong and healthy—able to do most of the more strenuous jobs around the farm—but not quite as bright as Gerry. This wasn't meant to be a put-down, it was just the way Mom and Dad saw the two of us.

However their opinion became my belief. As I grew up, I accepted the idea that Gerry was smarter than me as a fact of life, not because of anything he did or I did not do, but because it was what my parents thought. I now know that this happens a lot and it is not always true. Maybe you've accepted other people's opinions about you without question as well. Be careful how often you do that. Other people are not always right.

Like all farm kids, Gerry and I had chores to do every day. These included feeding the livestock—we had pigs, cows, horses and chickens—and keeping the pens, stalls, coops, and pigsties up to Dad's demanding standards of cleanliness. It was boring, tiring, dirty work and I resented the fact that I usually was assigned the hardest jobs because I was considered to be the stronger. I always thought Gerry got the easy end of the stick.

During the summer, we also had to help with the work around the farm. Work was what you did after the daily chores were finished. It consisted of planting, watering, hoeing, weeding, and eventually harvesting the crops and was just as boring and tiring as doing chores; although I must admit it was not quite as dirty. We also had to kill, pluck, and clean the chickens, a job I hated more than any other.

As the crops ripened and were harvested, Dad and Gerry would load up the wagon at the end of each week and haul them to Toronto to be sold at the Farmer's Market along with the chickens we had prepared.

Gerry usually went with my father on these trips. I rarely did. My job was to stay at home and get the farm prepared for the next week's production. Every Saturday, as I helped load the wagon and watched Dad and Gerry drive away to the city, I grew more resentful. Sure I was the stronger one, but why did that have to mean that I got all the dirty jobs while Gerry had all the fun?

Even at home, Gerry got the best jobs. We had a small roadside fruit and vegetable stand where we sold whatever we picked to people passing by. We didn't have refrigerators or ice boxes so everything we picked had to be sold before it spoiled. Berries, in particular, didn't last long. Mom made jam with the fruit that couldn't be sent to Toronto. The rest had to be sold quickly or it would be thrown away and we wouldn't make any money on it.

At our fruit stand, a pint of berries sold for about 10 cents and those dimes were important to small truck farmers like us. They would pay for our essentials—groceries, clothes, and coal for the stove. Moreover, once these expenses were covered, there generally was not a lot left over for savings or the fun things that many of us take for granted now. (By the way, a pint of fresh berries sells for about $4.00 today. Times have changed!)

It was Gerry's job to run the fruit stand—selling produce to the passersby.

"What a cushy assignment that is," I thought. "All he does is sit in the shade of a big maple tree and shoot the breeze with the customers while I bend over in the hot sun all day to pick berries, clean them up, put them into baskets, and tote them out to the side of the road. What's wrong with this picture?"

I wanted Gerry's job. I wanted to sit at the stand during the day and to ride to the market in Toronto with Dad every Saturday. That's where the fun was. When was it going to be my turn?

Gerry and I were eight years old when one day I talked to Jim about asking Dad to let me help sell berries at the fruit stand. It was the summer of 1939—just before World War II broke out—and I had been picking raspberries for what seemed like forever.

Dad had to be persuaded that I was smart and careful enough to make the correct change for customers. He knew Gerry could do this but he wasn't sure about me. It took Jim and I a while to convince him to let me do it.

I was excited. It was the chance I had been waiting for. However as I was setting up the stand the next morning, negative thoughts began to pop into my head, scary thoughts like…

"What if I really am too dumb to do this?"

"What if I can't figure out the correct change when someone buys something?"

"What if Dad gets angry with me?"

"I'm scared."

"What if I fail?

"What if I fail?

"What if I fail?"

Have you ever had thoughts like this? I had them all through my childhood. These thoughts are known as *negative conditioning* and learning to deal with them involves changing these negative thoughts to positive ones. In this book, we're going to talk about that a lot.

Anyway, back to the roadside stand. There I was, all by myself, trembling with anticipation and fear. What if I can't do it? **What if I fail?**

On the counter was a crate of raspberries that Gerry had not sold the day before. The crate contained 36 pints of berries. At 10 cents a pint, that added up to $3.60—an enormous sum at the time. At $4.00 a pint, that crate of raspberries would be worth $144.00 in today's money. However if they weren't sold by the end of the day, they would have to be used to make jam—which would bring a lot less than $3.60.

It wasn't long before a sleek new car pulled over to the stand and a friendly-looking man and wife got out and came over to me. I wasn't sure if I should be excited or scared to death.

"How much are the raspberries?" he asked.

"Ten cents a pint," I replied.

"How much will you take for three pints?"

I hadn't counted on bargaining with him. He wanted a discount if he bought three pints and my math wasn't good enough to figure out how to take off 10 percent. After all, I was only eight!

"Why don't you buy the whole crate sir," I finally blurted out.

I think he was surprised that a little kid would suggest something like that because all he said was "How much?"

"Three dollars." (Actually I had given him more than 10 percent off, but I was too flustered to realize it at the time.)

"I'll talk it over with my wife. She's the one who's going to make the jam."

And after a few minutes, the deal was struck. The friendly-looking man gave me three one-dollar bills and my business career had begun!

Encouraged by the success of my first transaction, I sold the rest of the raspberries within the hour and headed back out to the field to pick more. My Dad was already there.

"I thought you were going to look after the fruit stand," he said.

"I sold the whole crate for $3.00," I said. "I need to pick some more."

I figured my Dad was impressed. Anyway, he never again worried about me making change or anything else about running the fruit stand. Because I sold all the raspberries and we didn't have to throw any away, his opinion of me had changed completely. As for me, my confidence soared. I proved that my parents' opinion of me was wrong. I was shrewd. I could cut a bargain. I could make a sale!

It was the first time I ever really believed in my abilities and it set the stage for me to accomplish things in life that I may not have even attempted otherwise. It showed me that I had the intelligence and capability to achieve goals, feel good about myself, and use my abilities to be successful.

If you have a dream, don't hesitate. Just do it! When your mind presents you with negative thoughts, don't pay attention. Just do it! Negative thoughts limit far too many people from even trying, much less achieving, things that will make them happy. Don't let this happen to you. Just do it! If I'd listened to all the negative comments made about me—he only has a ninth grade education; he didn't go to school; he's the dumb twin—I would never have gotten anywhere, much less be writing a book!

Just do it!

Walter D. Wintle was an American poet who lived in the early 1900s. Today almost nothing is known of him or his other works, but his name is remembered for this one poem:

If you think you are beaten, you are.
If you think you dare not, you don't.
If you want to win, but you think you can't,
It's almost a cinch that you won't.

> *For out in the world you soon will find;*
> *Success begins with a person's thoughts.*

*It's all in your state of mind.—[**I think there
must be another line to this stanza**]*

*Many a race was decided
Before it was ever run.
And many a battle was lost
Before it had even begun.*

> *Think big and your deeds will grow,
> Think small and you'll fall behind,
> But think you can and you will
> It's all in your state of mind.*

*Life's battles don't always go
To the stronger or faster man,
Sooner or later the ones who win
Are the people who think they can.*

Just do it!

Miss Hammil and My First Bank Account

Gerry and I started our formal education the way
most country kids did in the 1930s and 40s, in a two
room schoolhouse about a mile from our farm. All the
kids in grades one to four were taught in a single room
by the same teacher—Miss Myrtle Hammil.

I had a hard time adjusting to school life. For one
thing, I'm left-handed. Back in those days, you weren't
allowed to use your left hand for writing. It sounds
strange now, but back then left-handed kids were considered, "the devils children," and were forced to learn
to write with their right hands.

To get an idea of how difficult this was, try it for
yourself. If you are normally right-handed, try writing

with your left. If you're a lefty, try it with your right. It's not easy, is it?

Of course Gerry was right-handed so he had no problem. I, on the other hand, had an awful time. My right hand just didn't connect with my brain the same way my left hand did, and being forced to learn in such an unnatural way really mixed me up. When it came to writing, school wasn't fun.

However other things were fun. One day when I was in third grade, Miss Hammil had each student bring 25 cents to class. In the afternoon we all trooped over to a local bank to open savings accounts and deposit the money. Her purpose was to teach us that saving was important. After we had all opened our accounts, she urged us to make regular deposits and explained that the bank paid us interest on the money we saved so our wealth would increase even more.

It was a lesson I have never forgotten. I think the habit of saving money is one that every kid needs to acquire as early in life as possible.

School Days

During our elementary school days, you might say Gerry was a bit of a whiz kid while I was more of a fizz kid. He sat at the front of the room and I sat in the back where I wasn't trying to compete with him.

In 8th Grade, we both caught scarlet fever. I, being stronger, was able to throw it off without much trouble; but in Gerry the disease escalated into rheumatic fever—a much more serious condition—and caused him to miss so much school that he had to repeat the year.

It wasn't until the 10th Grade that I really started to come into my own. That was the year students could start choosing some of their own optional courses. I liked art and was pretty good at it. I also wanted to learn to type. So I chose a commerce course which included typing lessons and an art course. The school principal, however, insisted that I take Latin and French – courses that helped students prepare for university.

There was no way I was going to pass Latin and French, much less go to university. So, having just completed the 9th grade, I left formal schooling, never to return.

That doesn't mean I pooh-pooh education today. In today's complex world, education is essential and I encourage you—as I have encouraged each of my four children—to stay in school as long as you can.

Nowadays there are trade schools where you can learn to do the things I was good at—carpentry in particular. But those schools were not common back in the early 1940s, especially if you were only 17. After dropping out of high school I had to find a way to educate myself.

I apprenticed under a master carpenter and found out on my own how to use my talent to make the maximum return. I've been learning like that ever since, and I believe that I'll be learning continually for the rest of my life. My very first project would set the stage for everything that would follow.

A Home for My Parents

Ever since the 1930s, my parents had been living in that small bungalow without indoor plumbing; and now that I was trained and available, I resolved to design and build them a home that was more comfortable. And do it for free!

I thought it was going to be a once-in-a-lifetime project but my brother Jim and his wife also wanted a free house. Being family, I could hardly refuse their request so I designed and built their home, too.

The practical skills and confidence that I gained building these homes was invaluable. By the way, both are still standing. I spent about $8,000 on materials and sub-trades to build them in 1948 and they're now worth close to $500,000 each.

Remembering Miss Hammil

I apprenticed as a carpenter for four years, working on the side to make some extra money. Miss Hammil's lesson about saving money never left me. At the end of four years I had about $5,000 in the bank.

When my apprenticeship ended I decided to go into the contracting business on my own. With my savings, I bought three residential lots and found a financial company that would provide me with a mortgage to cover the cost of construction. Fortunately I was able to sell two of the houses before I finished building them. This process of starting to build a home before it has been sold is called speculative building, or "building on spec." Because I made a profit on the first two homes, I was able to complete the third one and sell it too.

Urbanization and the Building Boom

By the early 1960s, the towns around Toronto were growing at an amazing pace. It was a great time to be either a farmer or a home builder. The farmers sold their land to the developers and the developers provided houses and apartments to the people who were flooding into the area to commute to downtown Toronto.

I knew that many of the farmers who sold out to the developers would want to remain in the area. Like me, they had lived there all their lives. Over the course of about 15 years, I made a good living building houses, apartment complexes, and commercial buildings, to satisfy this demand.

I particularly remember one project. It began when the chairman of the local planning board invited me to his home one Saturday for coffee with him and his wife. I regularly appeared before the planning board to discuss my development projects and had gotten to know Mr. Shantz, a retired railroad executive who had moved to our community from Toronto some years earlier because he and his wife had always wanted to live away from the big city. They bought a small home with a white picket fence around the yard—one of the prettiest houses in town—within walking distance of church and friends.

During our visit, Mr. Shantz who was in his 70s, took me on a tour of the property that is located near the main street of the town of Markham, Ontario. To my great surprise, it turned out his house was situated on only a small portion of the entire estate. Out behind it a huge parcel of beautiful land opened up before me, with hundred year old trees and a ravine with a small stream dividing it into two parts of roughly equal size. There must have been about three acres in all and the grass was trimmed so it looked like a small golf course. I was astonished to find such an amazing piece of land right in the heart of our small town.

Back in the house I asked Mr. Shantz if he would allow me to buy the property if he ever decided to sell. He agreed and we shook hands on the deal. I was really excited about possibly owning that property and dreamed about it for over a year, until one day Mr. Shantz invited me over to view the property again. As we walked along the ravine, he told me he was ready to sell.

"I think you could build 50 suites on this site," he said. "Do you still want to buy it?"

"Of course I do," I replied, scarcely able to believe my good luck. We settled on a price of $25,000, with $2,000 down and the rest due in 18 months.

I had purchased the land but now I had to figure out how to design and build a 50-unit apartment building. I worked with a friend—Jack Shaw—who had designed all of the houses I'd been building for over a decade. Jack wasn't an architect himself, but he had a talent for design and had developed relationships with engineers and architects who would certify his work. As my partner, he would design the building and I would build it.

We spent a year getting ready to break ground. Developing an apartment complex takes time; you have to put together a detailed plan, get financing, and obtain approvals from local authorities before you can begin.

One of our apartments was designated especially for Mr. and Mrs. Shantz. They had originally planned to replace the house with the picket fence with a new dream home. I admired their spirit—both were in their mid-70s—but eventually persuaded them that it would be preferable for them to rent the suite of their choice in our new development. In time, the Shantz's relocated to a beautiful two-bedroom suite overlooking the ravine. They lived there happily for the rest of their lives.

Some time later I bought the property on which the Shantz's small house was located and built my own dream home on the site. My wife and I raised our family there and have lived there now for more than 40 years.

A Change of Plans

Developing the Shantz property was an enormous project for me at the time. Not only was it one of the largest and most expensive residential projects ever built in Markham up to that time, but it was also the first big project I had ever attempted. Up to this point, I'd just built single family homes—and only a few of them!

However everything was going according to plan. The planning, design, financing, and approvals had been completed on time and on budget. The site work and framing had been done. The wiring and plumbing were in. Everything was sailing along when one day my partner, Jack Shaw, came into my office and told me he wanted out.

It turned out that Jack did not approve of the way the interior work was being done. Let me explain: today builders use drywall to enclose the rooms of a residence. However back in the 60s, the technique used was called lathe and plaster. A lattice frame was nailed to the wall and covered with a two coats of plaster—a rough initial brown coat followed by a smooth, white coat that could be painted or covered with wallpaper.

Jack didn't like how the plastering was being done. He was always something of a perfectionist and this annoyed him so much that he couldn't get over it. He wanted out.

He also wanted the $25,000 he had originally invested in the project plus an additional $25,000 for the work he had done up to that point, $50,000 in all. That was a very large sum in those days.

What's more, Jack told me if I didn't buy him out he was going to sell his 50 percent share to someone else. Oh boy, that's all I needed—a major project with a partner I didn't know. Of course I tried to get Jack to stay but he'd made his mind up.

I had no idea where I was going to get the $50,000 to buy him out. And the negative voices inside my head were loud and clear:

"Nobody wants to be my partner."

"What am I going to do?"

"What if I go broke?"

"What if I fail?"

Eventually, after a talk with my lawyer, I arranged for the company that held the mortgage on the property to increase the amount of the loan by $50,000 to enable me to buy Jack out.

I became the sole owner of the apartment building and this set the stage for what came next.

Millionaire

Six months later, every one of the building's 50 suites was rented. Anyone in real estate will tell you that a zero vacancy rate is not only very desirable, it's rare. What's more, a fully-occupied apartment building is worth a lot more than a partially-completed one.

Everything had come up roses for me. By purchasing Jack's share of the building, I increased my ownership position from 50 to 100 percent. Because it was fully occupied, the building was now valued at $2 million. If I sold it, I would realize a profit of more than a million dollars after paying off the mortgage and other expenses.

And I was only 28 years old.

It was perhaps the best deal I ever made; and what made it even better was the fact that Jack and I remained friends. He continued designing houses for me for years. In the end, both of us got what we wanted.

The incident taught me things—about business and about myself. I learned that:

- It's possible to turn what appears to be a setback into a business opportunity;
- Honesty and integrity pay dividends. Treat your business associates the way you want to be treated and they will continue to support you if things get tough;
- Being rich is not about taking advantage of others. Being rich is about maintaining strong relationships with people you respect and who respect you.

I Change Jobs

In 1969, after building about 500 houses, apartment buildings, commercial, and industrial projects, I decided to go into the real estate business as a salesman. Having experienced considerable success as a builder,

I was confident I had the ability to master the many courses in law, economics, and business required to obtain a real estate license. My old fear of academic courses had long since vanished.

After obtaining my realtor's license I completed a two-year internship as a sales person working for a local broker. It was like being an apprentice again. However my real goal was to have my own company and in 1972, starting with two sales people, I opened Armour Real Estate Inc. We became part of the Century 21 group a few years later and while I had been trained in industrial and commercial leasing and investment properties, our bread and butter was residential property.

By the early 80s, we had become one of the best franchises in the Century 21 system. In fact from 1982 through 1984 we were the top producing Century 21 office in Canada. I was very proud of my team.

By 1994 we had some 75 agents working out of our office. One of the best of them, Jenny Cook, came to me one day with an offer to purchase the company. She and her husband wanted to go into business for themselves. I could understand their desire. When you work for someone else, there are limits to how far you are able to pursue your dreams. After all, you're an employee, not the boss. On the other hand, being in business for yourself frees you to go as far as your imagination and hard work will take you.

Where to go next? Well, I decided to get into the ski resort business. Our family had long belonged to the Skyloft Ski Resort northwest of Toronto. It was a place that held a lot of memories for us and I particularly enjoyed the sport and the lovely setting. When it came on the market, I decided to buy it and turn it into a four-season resort.

The resort needed a lot of work. It had been neglected for some time. However with my experience in construction and real estate development, I was just the person for the job. Oddly enough, the fact that I knew little about running a ski resort was not a problem. I'd taken courses in business administration and knew how create the essentials—vision and mission statements, business and marketing plans—and I had sufficient capital lined up to pay for the required upgrades. The basics of successfully running a profitable business are similar no matter what type of business it is; so I was confident that by hiring knowledgeable people to look after the day-to-day operations, I would be successful.

Skyloft Resort is located at the top of the Oak Ridge Moraine, an area of elevated land stretching from the town of Caledon in the west almost to the City of Peterborough in the east. The site offers a series of magnificent vistas. My plan was to add a golf course and about 50 houses to develop the property to its full potential.

However these ambitions were thwarted by an act of the Ontario government that prohibited new development in the area. There were a number of reasons for that, not the least of which was the fact that the Oak Ridge Moraine sat on top of an underground water source that fed Lake Ontario and Lake Simcoe.

The development restriction was a significant problem. Because of it, the resort was totally dependent on the ski trade for its revenue. In that part of southern Ontario, ski season lasts three or four months at best, so we were forced to do some creative marketing to get people to use the property for the remainder of the year.

Because it was such a beautiful location, we were able to rent out our main ski lodge for weddings and special events in the spring, summer, and fall. But it would never become the kind of all-season resort and residential project that I had envisaged going in. When, after 11 years, I had the opportunity to sell, I didn't hesitate. I don't regret buying it because we had many happy family times there and we all loved it. However, as my daughter Sarah never tired of reminding me, it was a service industry, not a real estate development which is where my heart truly lies.

That's how I just did it: life long learning, persistence, developing self confidence, and finding good people to work with. Now it's time to move on, to help you to *just do it*. However before I do, I want to introduce you to the most important principle I followed on my way to achieving financial success.

Paying Yourelf

George S. Clason was an American who wrote about how to achieve financial success. His simple stories were set in ancient Babylon and illustrated financial and moral principles. They were written to teach basic financial principles—lessons that are as relevant today as they were back in biblical times. Many of them were later complied into a book called *The Richest Man in Babylon*. I first read it when I was 16 and you can still buy it at bookstores today.

The premise of the Babylon Theory, as it is called, is that you should pay yourself at least 10 percent of any money you receive before paying anyone else:

He turned to an egg merchant and he set an example. He stated that if the egg merchant will choose only one basket and put each morning ten eggs but take out from it only nine eggs, and then what will happen? The egg merchant answered that it will overflow as time passed by.[1]

If you learn to live on 90 percent of your total income, you'll never miss the other 10 percent. Put it into a savings account and when you have enough, invest it. Never spend it.

The ten percent you invest continues to earn a return for you 24 hours a day. That's 8,760 hours a year. As an employee, you work 40 hours a week, or 2080 hours a year. That means your money works for you 6,680 hours a year more than you work for yourself.

If you start on your 25th birthday, by the time you retire at age 65, your money will have been working for you over 250,000 hours more than you've worked for yourself.

If you borrow money, you have to pay interest to someone else. When you pay yourself first, that interest comes to you. Doesn't it make more sense to invest money and have it work for you than to borrow money and continually pay interest?

I'll have more to say about this later in the book.

---

[1] *The Richest Man in Babylon—The Success Secrets of the Ancients*, by George S. Clason. Publisher—Signet/First published in 1926/ISBN 0451205367

What You Should Have Learned From This Chapter

❖ Don't believe negative thoughts about yourself.

❖ What you fill your mind with, you will be. Fill your mind with positive thoughts.

❖ Riches are best measured by the number of successful relationships you maintain, not by how much money you have.

❖ Walk your talk. Keep your commitments.

❖ Formal education is just the beginning. Keep discovering new ways to learn and you'll continue to grow in wisdom and competence.

❖ Make your savings account your lifelong financial partner.

❖ Save 10 percent of everything you receive.

DISCOVERING
WHO YOU ARE

Often we don't even realize who we're meant to be because we're so busy trying to live out someone else's ideas. But other people and their opinions hold no power in defining our destiny.

—Oprah Winfrey

In the last chapter, I discussed how my parents always thought my brother was smarter than me and how that affected my attitude towards school and colored the way I thought about myself. It was part of the reason I didn't do very well in school.

I was the physically strong one, the one who was expected to work with my Dad in the fields doing the chores. Gerry was the one who got to go to the Farmers Market with Dad every Saturday to do the work that required more intelligence than brute strength.

To tell you the truth, I resented it. I felt my parents expected me to end up as a laborer. I wanted more for myself than that. I wanted to be someone people could look up to. Above all, I wanted a better life than I'd had so far.

Though neither of us realized it at the time, it was my mother's desire to have electric lights in our home that proved to me you can choose to make life better. After years of reading by kerosene lamps, Mom decided that we were going to get electric lights. It was one thing that she really wanted and Dad wouldn't provide it for her. He thought electricity was a frivolous waste of money and would have none of it. So one time when Dad was away from home for a week or so, Mom had an electrician come out and wire the house—and put an extra light for him in the barn.

Dad came home to a farm that was lit up like a Christmas tree. I expected him to be very upset with Mom but to my surprise, he took it all very calmly. I think the light in the barn settled it for him.

Not only was it the first time I'd ever seen my mother stand up to my father, but it also showed me that anything was possible if you overcome your negative thoughts. Mom didn't know how Dad would react, and I'm sure that, deep down, she was afraid he might explode. But she acted in spite of her fear, ignored the negativity of what might be and embraced the possibility of what could be. Having electricity in the house changed our family life for the better.

Negative thoughts can play over and over in your mind, leaving you afraid to do even little things that will improve your life. By overcoming negative thoughts, you open the door to becoming anything you want to be—successful, wealthy, and happy.

So what do you fill your mind with? Whatever it is will determine your self-image—how you see yourself. And that will go a long way towards determining how successful you become.

Success is defined in many ways. How you define it will likely be different than how I define it. My idea of success was predicated on my ability to earn money. Yours may be predicated on helping others or something totally different. However we can agree on this: self-confidence is created by overcoming fear and embracing opportunity.

How Negative and Positive Language Shape Your Self-Image

People usually base their opinions of themselves on the things they heard when they were children. Think about the things your parents, friends and acquaintances said about you when you were very young. Were they positive—praise for the things you did well—or were they negative—putdowns that highlighted those things at which you were not so proficient? You know the putdowns I'm talking about: *You'll never amount to anything. You are not smart enough to do this or that.* And the most diabolical of them all, *why on earth do you think you could ever do that?*

Do you still hear those comments in your mind today? How have they affected your decisions, attitudes, and activities over the years?

Let me tell you something about negative talk: it has no basis in fact whatsoever. It's someone else's opinion of you, not your opinion of yourself. It is, in short, not true and if you allow that kind of talk to influence how you feel about yourself, you're likely to end up being less than you could be as a person.

It is strange but true that people seem to believe negative things more readily than they accept positives. Deep down, they are more willing to believe a statement like *you're stupid* than to believe *you're smart*. Why that is, I don't know.

When I was a kid and my parents told me I wasn't as smart as my brother, I believed them at first. But I eventually came to see that such beliefs were not going to get me anywhere. I took it upon myself to change those negative thoughts to more positive ones—*You can do it. You have talent. You are smart*—and my healthy self-image emerged as a result.

If you are a parent, I urge you to remember this: the words your child hears from you form the thoughts that shape your child's self image for the rest of his or her life. These words—positive or negative—will become embedded in their subconscious minds and form the basis of everything they believe about themselves.

I have often said that the potential for success lies within every person. So if someone says something negative about you, don't believe it. And don't try to argue with them .Thank them for their comment and move on, then teach your son or daughter to do the same thing.

The Power of Encouragement

A friend once told me that the greatest gift she could give to her children was encouragement.

"At bedtime every night, I would find something positive to say to them," she said. "It might have been something as simple as 'you did a great job brushing your teeth today' but I always found something."

Another friend told me that the last thing he said to his daughter every night for the first 10 years of her life was *I love you, I'm proud of you and you're precious to me.*

"She's over 30 now and her mother and I still write that on her birthday card every year," he said.

An important part of being a good parent is to encourage your children, treat them well, and let them know how much they mean to you. They'll hear many discouraging words as they grow up but what they hear from you will have the biggest impact on the kind of adults they eventually become. So while you work on eliminating negative mind chatter (that's what I call that negative voice inside your head) from your own life, make certain you continually provide positive mind chatter to your kids.

Whenever you can, remind your children how valuable they are to the world at large and to themselves. Although there are more than six billion people on Planet Earth, each of us has unique talents, gifts, and intelligence. As a parent, it is your duty to remind your children that they are special, free to go as far in life as their talent and drive will take them, and that they never have to settle for someone else's idea of success.

Growing up working on the farm I was always able to envisage what my next step would be and to believe that I could accomplish anything I set my mind to. Like everyone else, I occasionally faced roadblocks, but I was able to take advantage of the opportunities that these challenges always presented. You can too.

Our Mental Faculties and How They Work

To be a successful money manager and live an abundant life, you must first understand how your brain functions.

Most people recognize the terms "right-brain" and "left-brain" thinking. They refer to the parts of your brain that control certain abilities. The right side of the brain is creative, visual, and intuitive; while the left side is more factual and analytical.

In all, there are six primary mental faculties that work in concert with one another to direct your thoughts and actions. Knowing about these faculties will help your brain work more efficiently and effectively on your behalf. The six faculties are:

- **Perception**—the faculty that keeps you aware of what's going on around you and helps you understand and learn from it. As might be expected, your perception is primarily governed by your five senses—sight, touch, hearing, smell, and taste.

- **Reasoning**—the ability to make decisions based on analysis of the situation. Your mind combines the perceptions of your five senses with your past learning to come to a conclusion. Reason is you brain's judgmental faculty.

- **Memory**—the capacity to store and recall information from past experiences, judgments, and results. Your memory is the faculty that can prevent you from making the same mistake over and over again. Though some people seem to be able to access their memories better than others, each person can draw on the store of learning, experience, and thoughts that they accumulate over the course of their lifetime.

- **Intuition**—often described as "gut feeling." It's the faculty that allows us to instinctively know something without having to consciously reason it out. Sometimes experienced as déjà vu—the feeling that you've already experienced a situation that is new to you—intuition is the most mysterious of your mental faculties.

- **Will**—the power to make a decision and subsequently control events to achieve a desired outcome. It is also known as 'focus' and is characterized by perseverance, dogged determination, and a willingness to keep trying until you succeed.

- **Imagination**—the ability to create new ideas and images of things that have not yet come to pass. Dreams flow from your imagination. So does creativity. Great inventions and world-changing ideas all have their origin in someone's imagination. The world of imagination is sometimes referred to as your 'metaphysical reality.' It can be quite different from the physical and material reality that your five senses perceive but it plays an equally important role in helping you achieve a successful life.

These mental faculties are tools that are available for our use whenever we wish to take advantage of them. Like the five physical senses, the key to using them properly is first of all to be aware that they exist and apply them in ways that help you improve your self-image.

Your mind also has two other divisions—the conscious and the subconscious. Using your five physical senses, you take information into your conscious mind. At the same time, that same information is logged into your subconscious mind where it remains for the rest of your life. So those negative statements you may have heard when you were young will remain recorded in your mind along with everything else. And these negative thoughts have a nasty tendency to jump back into your conscious mind at the most inopportune times. That's the bad news.

The good news is that when these negative thoughts jump back into your conscious mind, they can be quickly replaced by positive thoughts if **you choose to do so.** So your job is to be alert. Don't allow yourself to become overwhelmed by negative thoughts. Replace them with positive alternatives as soon as you become aware of them. Do not dwell on negative thoughts.

Your Personal Paradigm
A paradigm is a framework of ideas and concepts that enables you to make sense of something. It's the lens through which you view the world. Each of us has a set of beliefs, assumptions, cultural norms, and practices that make us unique individuals. Your personal paradigm determines how you see things, and how you learn from the things that happen around you.

As someone who spent a long time in the construction business, I tended to see myself as the person who took what my designer, Jack Shaw, had in mind—in other words his paradigm—and translated it into a completed project. I assembled the materials required, contacted the tradesmen that I needed to hire, and set up the construction schedule so that the home, apartment complex, or commercial building could be completed on time.

Over the years—as new construction materials became available and construction methods became more efficient—building a house changed considerably. For example in the 1970s, the old technique of using a lattice frame covered with a plaster to finish the interior walls of a house gave way to pre-formed sheets of drywall. Because of that, I had to change part of my paradigm to incorporate this change.

But more importantly, my plasterers had to start thinking of themselves as drywallers if they wanted to stay in business. That required a shift in their business paradigm. There were, of course, some people who could not—or would not—make that paradigm shift and eventually the world passed them by.

The point of this story is that paradigms can, and often must, be changed. And changing your self-image is the first step in changing your personal paradigm.

So what will you fill your mind with? As Norman Vincent Peale said, "What you fill your mind with, you will be."

If you fill your mind with negative thoughts; if you constantly think about what is wrong with your life and why you can't have the happiness and fulfillment that you see in others, you need to create a new paradigm—a new self-image.

This book can help you discard your negative paradigm and replace it with a positive one—a paradigm of abundance, happiness, and satisfaction. To use another construction term, it can help you replace some of the faulty wiring—lack of self-confidence and negative self-image—that is limiting your chance for success.

Remember that "success begins with a person's thoughts" and you are free to choose whatever thoughts you wish to put into your mind.

Choose to make your thoughts positive and life-affirming; remember that success begins when you create a positive paradigm for you and your family. With that sort of a foundation to build on, you'll find it easy to develop the skills to become a richer you.

What You Should Have Learned From This Chapter

- ❖ What you have been told or have experienced determines how you see yourself.

- ❖ Choose to reject the negative statements of others. They are not the truth.

- ❖ Your self-image determines how you perceive yourself and often determines how much success you will have.

- ❖ What you fill your mind with determines your attitude towards life and it influences your behavior.

- ❖ Every child is special, with unique talents and abilities.

- ❖ As parents, it is important that we help our children develop a healthy self-image by praising and encouraging them as much as we can.

- ❖ Your six mental faculties—perception, reasoning, memory, intuition, will and imagination—are tools that can help you live a successful life.

3

KEEP YOUR EYES
ON THE PRIZE

*"Whether you think you can or you think you can't,
you're right."*

—Henry Ford

I didn't achieve my success as the result of years of
careful planning. I didn't analyze every step that I
took. In all honesty, in some of my first business
deals, I felt like I was flying by the seat of my pants.
I don't wish to downplay the importance of having a
business plan and doing your research, but, when I
look back at my achievements, I owe the majority of
my success to maintaining a positive attitude.

Business plans can fail, customers can change their
minds, and investors can pull out. You will never have
100 per cent of the control in these situations. What
you can control is how you react to adversity. Your attitude is the only thing that is up to you and only you.
I would argue that maintaining a positive attitude is

the most important factor in the success of any task. It may sound simplistic but you will be amazed at how much you can accomplish just by thinking you can.

A Lesson Learned

It was the end of a day on a hot, sticky Friday afternoon. The sweat was dripping off my face as I watched the other workers get in their cars and drive off to their families, leisure activities, and undoubtedly, a much better Friday evening than the one I was about to have. The excessive humidity was preventing the concrete from setting; I had been at work for ten hours and wouldn't be leaving anytime soon. The heat and the long hours were making me tired, cranky, and dreading the work that still had to be done, but I wiped my brow, took a deep breath and settled in for the long haul.

The sun had long since risen by the time the concrete had settled to my satisfaction. All I could think of was a cold shower and my nice, comfortable bed. I had gone over to my truck and was just about to open the door when a real estate agent showed up with a prospective buyer. Any other time this would have made me rejoice, but now it had me cursing under my breath. I was so tired. I had worked 24 hours straight to get this job finished. The buyer couldn't have picked a worse time to show up.

The agent asked me to show the buyer around the house. Annoyance was written all over my face as I took him from room to room, unenthusiastically answered the few questions he dared ask me. I rushed the agent and his client out of the house so I could get the rest I had more than earned.

After a good night's sleep I woke up in great spirits. The first thing that popped into my head was, "Great, I have an interested buyer. Maybe I'll be able to sell the house this week!"

On Monday, I ran into the real estate agent in a local coffee shop. Excitedly, I walked over to him and asked him what the buyer thought of the house I was building. I knew he would be impressed by the craftsmanship that had gone into it.

The real estate agent looked at me as if I had just insulted his mother. He slammed his cup of coffee down.

"He wouldn't buy your house if hell froze over!"

I was shocked. I regained my composure and managed to force out a quiet and confused, "Why?"

"The buyer said you were the rudest, most miserable person he ever met! He wouldn't buy a house from you if you were selling it for a nickel!"

My poor attitude had ruined a relationship with a customer. That was an important lesson for me and I'm glad I learned it early in my career. I chose to work 24 hours straight. I could have smiled through my tiredness and made the buyer feel comfortable but instead I chased him away. I was focused on going home and getting some sleep. I got the sleep but lost the sale. The episode taught me that no matter what you focus on, you will usually get it.

A good attitude is the vehicle that will take you to that success no matter what you want to achieve. If you walk around telling yourself nothing good will ever happen to you, what kind of effect do you think that will have on your life? More importantly, what do you think your kids will learn from it? A bad attitude is a major roadblock that can make the difference between a life of dreaming about having something and a life of doing something about it.

The Science of Success

By simply saying we can achieve something, we substantially improve the likelihood of our success. When we think we can't do something, we might as well give up, as the possibility of success plummets to almost zero. Like so many things in life, our brains prefer the path of least resistance. If we consistently think positive thoughts, our brain becomes skilled at creating more positive thoughts. If we consistently think in a negative manner, our brain becomes skilled at creating more negative thoughts. The science behind this is called neuroplasticity, the study of the brain's ability to change in response to experiences and thoughts. If we spend every day thinking negative thoughts and saying we can't do something, our brain moulds to this thought pattern and it becomes harder to form positive thoughts. In extreme cases, such as in depression, it becomes almost impossible to form positive thoughts.

Luckily, the therapy needed to fix this problem doesn't involve medication. Active positive thinking is what is needed to reform the brain so that it becomes better at forming positive thoughts. You must simply spend time focusing on what you can do rather than on what you can't.

How can we use neuroplasticity to become more successfully financially? It sounds complicated but it really isn't. Take the statement "I can't." Change it to "I can."

That's all. Rather than conceding failure at the first sign of difficulty, take a moment and ask yourself, "What do I need to do to make this work?" Then tell yourself, "I will make this work." Even if you don't really believe it, just say it. Say it to yourself and over time it will become easier and easier to rewire your thinking.

Overcoming Fear

An interesting thing happens once we get close to reaching our dreams, especially those dreams we had been told were too difficult to achieve. Fear begins to kick in. The question, what if I fail, begins echoing around in our heads until it becomes deafening. It feels like we're a kid again, worrying about the rest of our classmates laughing at us if we step outside the circle and try something original. So we tell ourselves, "You can't do this. Stop before you embarrass yourself!" It was exactly this fear that kicked in when I told my father I was going to sell the berries at the road stand. As soon as I was ready to do something outside my comfort zone, fear kicked in. "What if I make a mistake? What if I can't do it?"

When you find yourself following that path of thinking, stop. Say to yourself, "Do it now!" It's true, you might fail on your first, second or even third attempt. But, if you keep trying you will succeed. Always remember that. Simply by trying, you increase your chance of success by 100 percent.

Mastering Mistakes

No matter how much education or experience you have, you will make mistakes. Mistakes are a part of learning. As far as I'm concerned, the only mistake not worth making is failing to act. You can't expect to do everything perfectly the first time you try.

When you hear the name Henry Ford, you likely think of a success. What most of us don't know is that Henry Ford failed five times before he started the Ford Motor Company.

Ever hear of a business called Traf-O-Data? Likely not, but I'm sure you have heard of Microsoft. Bill Gates failed in his first business but later went on to revolutionize the way we use computers.

Thomas Edison's teachers told him he wasn't intelligent enough to do anything important. Luckily, for us, he didn't listen. He invented the light bulb after 1,000 failed attempts. Despite making mistakes that would make most of us give up, Edison said, "I haven't failed. I've found 1,000 ways that don't work."

All of these people succeeded because they didn't stop at the first signs of failure. You will make mistakes. Celebrate your mistakes because they are such an important part of success. If you go through life without making mistakes, you're not reaching high enough. If we refused to try something unless we could do it perfectly, none of us would have learned to walk.

The Power of Positive Thought

Do you ever wonder about people who manage to keep a smile, even through the worst of times? I used to look at these people and think there was something wrong with them. I came to the conclusion that they must be out of touch with reality; they must be ignoring the problems around them. We all go through bad times. The difference between those who maintain a positive attitude during tough times and those who don't is not blindness to adversity. The difference lies in acknowledging the problem and then telling yourself you will get through it. Remember, there's a difference between sadness and hopelessness. I try to say, "I know I can get through this. Stay calm. This will pass." Try to develop some affirming statements of your own to rely on even when times get tough.

Most exercise and diet plans tell you to keep a journal. This is because you are then accountable for the decisions you make regarding your health. A journal also allows you to celebrate your good days and keep track of what works and what doesn't. I do this with my success in business. When things aren't going my way, I can look at my journal and remind myself of my accomplishments. It helps me remember that I have achieved great things in the past and it motivates me to continue on my path of success. A journal is a great exercise to do with your spouse or your kids. A journal helps you set goals. And when you reach them, you can celebrate as a family. Encourage your kids to share and write down their successes. This gives them evidence that they are able to achieve anything they set out to do.

First You Sow. Then You Harvest.
I learned my first lessons in business growing up on the farm. If I wanted a nickel to go buy an ice cream,

my father would usually assign a chore, usually weeding the strawberry patch, before I was given the nickel. I learned I needed to lay the groundwork before I earned the reward.

One spring my father taught my siblings and me about growing flowers. He gave us seeds and showed us the best place to plant them. We made sure they got enough sun and water. Patiently, we waited for our flowers to grow. Finally they were ready to be trimmed, bunched, and sold at the Farmers Market. Growing the flowers taught me that success doesn't come overnight. In order to succeed, you must be patient. We could have tried giving the flowers more water and placing them in a sunnier spot but that wouldn't have done anything to speed up the process, in fact it would have eliminated any chance of our flowers reaching the market.

It seems that our world has become more and more focused on instant gratification. We don't want to wait for our reward. We want it now! Remember, anything worth achieving will take time. My father taught me this by giving me a handful of seeds and showing me what they could become with a bit of care and patience.

Whether you choose to grow flowers or to pursue a different goal, take the time to teach your children about the importance of patience and laying the groundwork before you earn the reward.

What do YOU Want?

If you asked 100 people what their idea of success is, you would likely receive 100 different answers.

Success is a relative concept. Admittedly, this book focuses mostly on professional and financial success, but happiness is attained when we feel successful in many areas of our lives. This is why it's so important to define success in other than financial and professional terms. If you think that simply having more money will make you a success, you may feel disappointed when you attain that goal. Also if you focus only on making more money, you might miss out on the other important things in life. Some people say success is getting a great paying job and an education.

What do you want your life to look like? Do you want to work for yourself? Do you want more time off with your family? Do you want a better position at your company? Talk about what your idea of success is with your children. Encourage your children to develop their idea of success. This will give your family focus and allow you to achieve your idea of success.

Attitude is Everything

No matter what you are trying to achieve in life, your mind will be either your main asset or your greatest liability. If you approach a difficult task with the attitude that you will do what you set out to do, you have a great chance of succeeding. Don't ever approach it half heartedly. Believe in yourself. Tell yourself you will succeed. Have patience. If you do this, nothing can stop you.

What You Should Have Learned From This Chapter

❖ Your self-image is closely tied to your attitude.

❖ Having a positive attitude will take you further than having a negative attitude.

❖ Whether you adopt a positive or negative attitude is up to you.

❖ You can consciously decide to change your attitude from negative to positive.

❖ Adopting a positive attitude is the first step on your road to success.

❖ Success is most often achieved by people who learn from their mistakes.

❖ Your thoughts will become your reality.

❖ There really is a Law of Attraction. Put it to use for you.

SUCCESS FACTOR#1
Overcoming Obstacles

"Obstacles don't have to stop you. If you run into a wall, don't turn around and give up. Figure out how to climb it, go through it, or work around it."

—Michael Jordan

In the next five chapters I will tell you about the five success factors I have used to achieve my goals. They're not complicated and I have used them again and again with amazing results.

Overcoming Obstacles

One of the major differences between those who succeed and those who don't is how they approach obstacles. Some reach an obstacle and give up saying, "Oh well, it just wasn't meant to be." Others look at the same obstacle and instead of seeing an end they see an opportunity. They see a way around.

I knew a fourteen-year-old-boy who had dreamed of designing and building homes and offices since he was eight years old. He knew that in order to do this he would need to go to university to study to be an architect. His parents feared they wouldn't have enough money to send him to college. They didn't encourage him towards his dream of becoming an architect. At that point, I'm sure many of us would understand if the boy had decided to give up. It would make sense if he decided to envision something easier, something his parents could support. But he didn't.

After much thought, the young man realized he could start making money mowing lawns for his neighbors. He had enough money saved up to buy a used lawnmower. He learned how to maintain the machine from the father of his friend. He made sure he was on time for each job and paid close attention to the quality of his work. His neighbors were so impressed that they started referring him to other people. Some of the jobs were very far away and he didn't have a driver's license so he would walk, sometimes more than a mile, to get to the jobs.

The boy knew that his lawn business would end once the cold weather hit so he started coming up with ideas that would generate money in the winter. In the fall he raked leaves and helped winterize gardens. By the time the first snow hit, the boy had saved up enough money to buy a snow blower. Rather than being stopped by the obstacle of weather, he seized the opportunity to start a new business. Getting work was easier this time, as he had built up a client base through mowing lawns. His customers trusted him. When he told them he would be offering snow removal, they readily accepted the service.

Going into the second summer, he could no longer keep up with all the work that came his way. He invested in two new lawnmowers and hired a friend who would help him manage the demand. He passed his driver's exam and bought a used truck so he would be able to get to jobs faster and be able to earn more money. He kept working and expanding his business. After he graduated from high school, he had saved up enough for the first two years of university.

Before he left for school, he sold his business to a competitor and was thus able to pay for his final year of college. He is now a successful businessman. He achieved this success using the strategies that you will be learning in the next five chapters.

How many times do you think that boy wanted to give up on becoming an architect? When his parents wouldn't support him? When he didn't have transportation to get to his jobs so he had to walk? When the cold weather hit, eliminating his lawn business?

Obstacles are relative. You might think something is impossible but if you shift your perspective, that same roadblock may not seem so bad. By seeing opportunities where others see obstacles, you greatly increase your chances of success.

Physical obstacles can usually be approached a number of ways. Two people come to a river. One turns back because the water is too deep and swift. The other sees a perfect opportunity to build a bridge.

One of the biggest obstacles I overcame was the fact that, at the age of fifteen, I was basically uneducated. My brother Gerry seemed much smarter than me and excelled in school. I always felt less next to him. My parents were so proud of his academic achievements. What could I possibly offer?

However instead of giving up, I decided to investigate other educational opportunities that would work for me. I went to trade school and learned carpentry. I found people I could learn from, including the master carpenter I apprenticed with. As I became more confident in my skills as a carpenter, I overcame my lack of education and instead used that obstacle as an opportunity to find a trade that would fit me well.

A common obstacle to becoming rich is the fear of having to manage money. Some think that investing and credit are too difficult to understand so they choose not to bother and merely get by. Some might feel that this is good enough, but financial savvy or the lack thereof, passes from generation to generation. You might think merely getting by is good enough for you, but do you think it is good enough for your children?

What You Should Have Learned From This Chapter

❖ Obstacles may contain the seeds of opportunities.

❖ How you look at an obstacle can show you how to turn it into an opportunity.

❖ Successful people face challenges and learn from mistakes.

5

SUCCESS FACTOR#2

Good Decision-Making
Leads to Success

Vacillating people seldom succeed. Successful men and women are very careful in reaching their decisions, and very persistent and determined in action thereafter.

—L. G. Elliott

It may sound simplistic but in order to be successful, you need to make good decisions. I talk about how mistakes are such an important part of success because it's usually in making mistakes that we learn to make good decisions. We have trouble learning how to make good decisions if we are afraid of making mistakes.

We can learn how to make good decisions from mentors—parents, teachers, or friends. Without a mentor you may have to learn through trial and error. However, not having someone to learn from doesn't mean you can't learn to make good decisions on your own.

Books are another resource. If you're looking to make a decision in a certain field, read about someone who has been successful in that field and find out what he or she did.

I've included the guidelines I have used for making good decisions. They have helped me replace my poor decisions with good ones. I know they can do the same for you.

Influencing Factors

Every decision you make is influenced by your past experiences, values, beliefs, and other external sources. Understanding what these sources are will help you make good decisions.

Values

Values are what you deem to be ethical or important. Values can be individual—such as a personal belief in equality—or societal, such as Canada's system of democracy.

Peers

Your peer group is made up of your co-workers, friends, and those who are the same age or standing as you.

Habits

Habits are formed throughout life. Habits such exercising and healthy eating can help you; habits such as smoking might hurt you.

Feelings

Feelings are how you react emotionally to things. For some, feelings are a moral compass. You know you are doing something you don't agree with when it makes you feel sad or uncomfortable. On the flip side, you know you are making a good decision when it makes you feel happy.

Ego
Your ego is your sense of self. Ego is very important because it gives you a sense of self-worth. However ego can be also portrayed in a negative light. An over-inflated ego leads to a person being self-righteous.

Family
When we think of family, most of us think of parents, siblings, and grandparents. But the definition of family is rapidly changing to include those people who have played an important role in your life and whom you know you can count on.

Risks and Consequences
Risk is the chance of loss. Consequences are the outcome of that loss. When making a decision, it's important to ask yourself if you can live with the consequences if you lose. By knowing your risks, you have the chance to reduce them.

Age
Age influences your decisions. When you are young you have less fear and less responsibility so your decisions don't seem as big. As you age you learn more about the risks of your decisions. You also have more decisions to make.

Making Your Move
Use the following list of statements to help you make good decisions.

1. The decision I want to make presents me with a series of options. These options are:
2. My research regarding each of these options suggests that:
3. I prefer the following option:
4. I prefer it because:
5. I have made a similar decision before and have learned that:
6. My wife, partner, kids, parents, etc. would prefer that I make the following decision:
7. My preferred decision will affect the following people:
8. If my preferred decision causes consequences, they are known to be:
9. To my knowledge, the negative effects of making this decision are:
10. I will make the following decision by the following date:

To start, use this list to make a simple decision such as where you want to go on vacation. This will allow you to become comfortable with the formula so you can use it to help you with major decisions.

Keeping a record of your decisions will allow you to review your decision-making process. Get your family involved. When you make a decision that doesn't work, go back in your records and find out what could have been done differently. When you make a good decision, write it down so it can help you to duplicate its success.

What You Should Have Learned From This Chapter

❖ Making good decisions is important, no matter what your age.

❖ Before you make a decision, consider all the information that's available to you.

❖ Following the 10 decision-making statements will help you uncover the things you need to learn when you make decisions.

❖ Successful people make daily decisions that lead to success.

CHAPTER

6

SUCCESS FACTOR#3

Goalsetting Helps You Get What You Want

Goals are the fuel in the furnace of achievement.

—Brian Tracy

I attribute most of my success to setting goals. Without goals we have no idea where we want to go. We can make a lot of mistakes along the way if we don't have a clear idea of the direction we're heading.

Setting goals is fun. Goals allow you to dream. They allow you to move past what you think are your limits and imagine what you really want. Do you want to make one million dollars a year running your own business? Do you want to create more time with family and less time at work? Do you want to work less so you can volunteer for community projects that are meaningful to you? Do you want to invent the next big thing?

Dream big. So often we are told to reign in our goals because they are impossible. We are told to be realistic because dreaming leads to unrealistic expectations. When we are young we feel we can be anything: a firefighter, a doctor, an astronaut. As we grow up, the possibilities seem to diminish. Don't let your possibilities diminish. Dream big. Impossible is simply a perception.

Goals

Goals are something to work towards achieving. Goals can be professional: I want that promotion. Or goals can be athletic: I want to run a seven-minute mile.

Goals can take days, months, years, or a lifetime to achieve. I'll tell you a secret; successful people set goals. I would be willing to guarantee that anyone you consider a success has his or her five-year goals written down. Most will have written down their lifetime goals.

Goals can be broken down into three categories:

–Short-term goals (one to four weeks)

–Medium-term goals (two to twelve months)

–Long-range goals (one year or longer)

Goals are described in short statements. I want to do ten chin-ups. I want to get a Masters Degree in Biology. I want to be the CEO of my company.

The most successful goals have the following elements:

Present Tense

Emotional

Realistic

Measurable

Action-based

That spells **PERMA**, which is short for permanent.

Here are some PERMA goals.

"I'm so excited that I made the honor roll for the spring semester."

"I am so grateful that we have paid off all of our debt and can now start saving for retirement."

"I am so excited to drive my new boat which I paid for with the money I made on my investments."

Present Tense
When we think of goals we usually think future tense. "I will get that promotion." "I will be in better shape." When we change the goal to present tense it becomes more believable. Suddenly the goal doesn't seem so far off.

Use "I am" not "I will be."

Use "I know" not "I will know."

Use "I have" instead of "I will have."

Emotional
It's important to include feelings as part of our goals. It's easier to do something when we know it will make us feel good. We're more likely to sacrifice that piece of pie if we have written about how great eating healthy makes us feel. It's easier to sacrifice a short-term reward when we know it creates a more fulfilling future.

Realistic
We talked about not limiting yourself when setting goals so you might be wondering why I am now telling you to be realistic. I'm not talking about realism in

terms of limiting your larger goal such as becoming the CEO of your company. But, if you leave your goal at that, you might feel a bit lost as you try to work towards it. So when you set a big goal, also set a series of smaller goals that will help you achieve your main goal. If you want to become a CEO, a smaller goal could be, "I will learn about my company's target markets this week so I am better prepared for my new responsibility."

Measurable

A measurement gives you something to grasp. Include numbers in your goal. For example, "I'm so happy I bought my car by saving $10,000." "I'm so thrilled to be ready for my marathon after six weeks of intense training."

Action-Based

By including an action in your goal, you give your brain an understandable activity. "I pay $10 a week into savings so I can save for retirement." "I go for a walk every day so I can lose five pounds."

Include others in your goal. If you make your goal about more than just you, you give yourself more reasons to attain that goal. "I am paying off our debt so I can take my family on vacation." "I am working from home two days a week so I can pick my children up from school."

I've created a construction business, a real-estate business, and a ski resort. Guess what? Each one of these successes came from setting goals. Each of these goals took time and effort to achieve.

You can learn how to set goals at any age. Begin by knowing what is important to you. Then brainstorm what you want to achieve. You can do this as a family.

In order to be successful in goal-setting you must use what works for you. Trying to fit in a goal-setting session on a night when your children have a soccer game isn't likely to work. If it is difficult to find time to get together as a family to set your goals, keep a journal where each member of your family can write his or her individual goals. Then schedule a goal-setting night once a month. Make it a priority and make it fun.

Although you will probably come up with multiple goals, pick one that you will particularly focus on achieving. By selecting a single goal, you increase your chance of success. Once you have your goal picked out, be ready to completely commit to it. Write down your goal and post it in your home in a place everyone will see it a number of times a day. Decide on a reward that your family will receive once you have reached your goal. You earned it.

What You Should Have Learned From This Chapter

❖ Pursuing goals provides you with direction.

❖ Achieving goals provides you with success.

❖ Every goal begins as an idea.

❖ The more passionate you are about a goal, the more likely you are to achieve it.

❖ Total success requires total commitment.

❖ Establish mini-goals as milestones to achieving your overall goal.

❖ Celebrate your success

SUCCESS FACTOR#4

Keeping the Faith

With ordinary talent and extraordinary perseverance, all things are attainable.

—Thomas Foxwell Buxton

Growing up on the farm taught me a lot about perseverance. I had to do a lot of tasks I didn't enjoy and I knew that if I didn't finish my work, Dad would send me back to complete the job. This taught me the importance of seeing a task through from start to finish whether it was cleaning the pigsty, or hoeing the garden. Now, I persevere because I want to achieve my goals. I know that good things don't happen without hard work and I also know the work is worth it.

When I was 21 years old I was invited to join a local Kiwanis Club, which had about 20 members. At the beginning of my second year I was elected the Ways and Means Chairman, and was put in charge of creating a project that would help my club raise money.

The Lions Club was well-established in our neighborhood, but the Kiwanis Club was fairly new. We were in competition to raise money in our small town and most people were used to giving to the Lions.

I came up with an idea to sell packages of mixed nuts that would be delivered one week before Christmas. I proposed the idea at our weekly meeting.

Instead of the approval I was expecting, I was shot down by everyone in attendance. The Lions sold chocolate covered nuts for Christmas and everyone said there was no way anyone would buy from the Kiwanis Club.

Feeling rejected, I went to the nut company in Toronto and spoke with a representative. He suggested we sell Licorice Allsorts so people would have a choice. I was excited. By offering variety, we might actually be able to increase sales in our town.

Full of hope, I made another presentation and was nearly booed out of the room.

"No one will want to buy Licorice Allsorts at Christmas," said the other members. "We'll look like fools."

I was ready to give up on the Kiwanis Club. I didn't need to volunteer my time just to be rejected. Walking out of that room and never looking back seemed like a great idea.

However rather than quit, I decided to see if my plan would work. I loaded up my car with Licorice Allsorts and mixed nuts and drove around the neighborhood. But I couldn't make myself get out of the car.

"No one will buy from you. You'll look like a fool," echoed in my head.

Finally, I tried something I had learned at a seminar. I rolled my window down and threw my keys out onto the yard of a potential customer. Now I had to get out of the car, if only to pick up my keys. Whether I would go to the person's door was another matter. I walked up the driveway, picked up my keys, took a deep breath, and kept walking.

I did this for the second and even the third house. Each time the response was the same: "No, I'm sorry we buy from the Lion's Club." Maybe everyone on the Kiwanis committee was right.

Disheartened, I walked back to my car and ripped open a package of the nuts and licorice. If I wasn't going to sell any of the treats, I might as well indulge. The licorice and the nuts were delicious and I suddenly realized I had been approaching my neighbors in the wrong way. More confident now, I walked up to another door.

"I know you probably buy from the Lion's Club, but we at the Kiwanis Club are offering mixed nuts and Licorice Allsorts," I said offering the box. "You won't have to pay for them until a week before Christmas. Here, try some. Which do you prefer? How many boxes would you like to buy?"

In an hour and a half, I had sold more than 150 boxes.

As you might guess, my next presentation to the Kiwanis Club went much better than the first two. The club accepted my idea and that Christmas we made more than $2,500 profit from the sales. It was a great lesson in the power of perseverance. I had no support from my community or my club. I had even begun to doubt my idea.

I'm so happy I rolled down my car window on that frosty night and threw my keys out the window. I'm so glad I persevered. In hard times, I've often thought back to that experience and whenever I need a bit of a kick to get going, I just remind myself to "roll down the car window, throw my keys out, and see what happens." The worst thing that will happen is people will say no. That's far less scary to me than having to admit that I never tried.

What is Your Motivation?

What will you do to motivate yourself? How will you persevere? What will get you through the hard times when it seems everyone around you is saying no?

Perseverance is the difference between setting your goal and achieving it. Think back. Think about the times you succeeded. Now think about the times you gave up. What do you think would have happened if you had kept trying? Don't give up. Keep trying.

What You Should Have Learned From This Chapter

❖ Perseverance is the difference between setting your goal and achieving it.

❖ Successful people persevere until they achieve their goals.

❖ Whatever it is, see it through to the end.

❖ Learn to use what motivates you to persevere and use it to achieve your goal.

❖ Teach your children the power of perseverance.

8

SUCCESS FACTOR#5

Seeing Success in Your Mind's Eye

Envisioning the end is enough to put the means in motion.

—Dorothea Brande

When I really want something, I try to imagine that it already happened. I think of my goal and I close my eyes. I think about everything that involves me reaching that goal. I think of what I will do and the others that will be involved in my success.

Visualization allows your brain to rehearse before the main event. It trains your mind to look for success and seize it. I've used visualization in all aspects of my life. I've used it to lose weight. By using visualization, I went from weighing 198 pounds to weighing 180 in twenty-one days.

I even used visualization to close a multimillion dollar deal.

About fifteen years ago, I was approached by one of the members of an investment club I belonged to. He was selling his golf course and wanted my advice. Although I specialized in residential sales, I happily gave him whatever guidance I could offer.

Over the next week, I couldn't forget our conversation. I knew I was letting an opportunity go by. I also knew that I was letting it go because of fear. I realized that I really wanted to sell that golf course. It was a challenge and I knew I could do it. I decided that it was going to be me who would sell that golf course.

I was at ground zero. I wasn't a golfer. I couldn't think of one possible buyer. I decided to go in small steps. First, I learned everything I could so I would be able to answer any questions prospective buyers might have.

But after that I hit a wall. I had no idea who to approach to buy the golf course. I decided I would give visualization a try.

Over the next two years I put visualization to work. I would find a quiet place to think about selling the golf course. I imagined a group of people in my office getting ready to transact the deal. I could see their faces. I could even imagine what they were wearing. I imagined them accepting the exact amount my friend wanted for the golf course.

At that time I was involved in building a 48 unit condo development located near a lake. I decided to buy a powerboat that I could use to take interested buyers on short tours. The boat had a navigation system called a "Loran C." I didn't know anything about how to use it so I called a real estate broker friend of mine who was a boater. I knew he was familiar with the equipment. He invited me to lunch in Toronto where he would teach me all about it.

Before he hung up the phone he asked me, "By the way, do you know if there are any golf courses for sale in your area?"

I was shocked. I quickly recovered and smiled as I said into the phone, "As a matter of fact, I do."

I couldn't believe it. Out of nowhere a friend of mine had inquired about the exact property I was trying to sell. But maybe it wasn't out of nowhere. Maybe visualization had paid off.

The buyer and the seller met in my office, exactly the way I had pictured it. Within four hours the deal was finished. The golf course sold for $43,750,000. This was the exact price I had wanted.

That was the largest sale I ever completed, and I truly believe I owe it to visualizing my success.

Visualization 101

As you did with your other goals, get a notebook and write down what you want. Keeping a record is important because it keeps you accountable.

Think about something you've wanted and then fill in these statements:

When I am successful, I will be wearing…

When I am successful, I will have…

When I am successful, I will be doing…

Choose one of your dreams. Then sit down and, just as I imagined the sale of the golf course, imagine your dream coming true. Imagine everything that surrounds your dream. Think in pictures.

For example, imagine buying the car of your dreams. Imagine having enough money to buy it. Imagine going to the dealership. What does the dealership look like? Now imagine your car, the exterior, the new leather seats, and the sound system. See yourself writing the check for the amount you saved. Imagine the salesperson giving you the keys. Then imagine the feeling as you drive that car for the first time.

Summary

You can use visualization for anything you want. Pick your dream and imagine it coming true. Get your family involved. Kids are often better at visualizing than adults because they have great imaginations. Reactivate your imagination. If people tell you to stop dreaming, ignore them, close your eyes, and imagine what you want coming true. It will.

What You Should Have Learned From This Chapter

❖ A positive self-image is closely linked to the ability to visualize success.

❖ If you can visualize your goal, you can achieve it.

❖ Take the time to visualize one of your goals twice a day for a month. Once you see yourself being successful, you will be.

❖ Visualize only what you want, not what you don't want.

❖ Help your kids learn to visualize too.

9

MANAGING YOUR MONEY

I believe managing is like holding a dove in your hand. If you hold it too tightly you kill it, but if you hold it too loosely, you lose it.

—Tommy Lasorda

Today it's probably more important than ever before to teach our children about money management. Every day we receive countless messages about spending now and paying later and it's landing us in a heap of trouble. Money management isn't complicated. But it does require attention and practice. I want to show you how you can use money management to: a) reach your financial goals and b) teach your children about money management so they are prepared for financial success.

Children, even very young ones, can learn the concepts of money management. Did you have a piggy bank when you were young? I'm guessing you did. Maybe you saved every penny until you could buy a new bike. A piggy bank is a tool you can use to teach a young child about the value of savings. Come up with a goal with your child for what she will do with her piggy bank savings. Then you can work together to reach her goal. This is a very basic lesson in savings. I will also go over other options for saving where your money will actually make you money. Once you understand this concept you will be able to pass the knowledge on to your children.

Finances may be the last taboo subject in our society. Most of us wouldn't dream of telling our friends how much we make. Sharing financial information may feel wrong because we view it as such a private matter. I understand this. I am not advising you to share private financial information that isn't appropriate for your children. But I do want you to talk to your children about money. I want you to absorb the information in this chapter, and work through the activities so you can share what you learn with your children.

I tried to pass the lesson of money management on to my daughters. Watching me, they learned the importance of saving. I thought that leading by example was enough. I now wish I would have taught them more about what money management is and their options for saving. My children are my inspiration to give other parents the tools to help their children flourish.

I knew one parent who used the game Monopoly to teach her children about money management. While they were playing a game of Monopoly on Friday, the woman's little boy asked about buying a toy he really wanted. The mother said she couldn't afford it this week.

"Why not?" questioned the little boy. "Don't you still have checks in your checkbook?"

Right then, that mother realized she needed to go beyond the game of Monopoly to teach her kids about money.

She gave each of her children $1,000. She then asked her children what they would buy first with the money.

The little boy piped up, "I want to buy my toy."

He took the money he would need to buy his toy from the stack of $1,000 and put it aside. His mother then explained what they needed to pay for every month.

"We need to pay these bills first," she explained as she wrote out the amounts of their monthly bills. "We also need to make sure we have enough money to buy groceries."

The boy looked sadly on as all the money was allocated to different areas. He was starting to understand that he would have to take the money he set aside for the toy as they would need it to pay the bills.

Disheartened, the little boy said, "I'm never going to be able to buy my toy."

The mother suggested that they could take a small portion of the money and put it aside in savings. That way, they could set aside a little bit of money each month until they had enough money to buy the toy. The little boy's face brightened as he put a small amount of money in an area marked savings.

A child who doesn't understand money management will likely turn into an 18-year-old calling you in a panic at the end of the month saying, "Mom, I can't make rent!" or "Dad, the power got cut off. What do I do?" Teach your children about money before they move out. If you give them the tools to understand their finances, your children won't need to borrow money from you at the end of each month.

The Secret of the Rich

Wealthy people pay themselves first. It's that simple. Instead of paying everyone around them first until they have nothing left, the rich always set aside a portion for themselves. By doing this, they guarantee that they will have money in the future. They are able to invest that money so it makes more money for them. Every penny you invest will work for you, even when you aren't working. Investments never take a day off. Think about it, the average person works forty hours a week. Invested money works twenty-four hours a day, seven days a week. When you work it out, your money works for you 104 more days a year than you do.

You don't need to be rich to start paying yourself first. Start by putting away 10 percent of your income into savings. Use the 90 percent that's leftover to pay your other costs. This might feel impossible at first. Just do it! It will force you to look at where you are spending your money and you will make adjustments until paying yourself that 10 percent becomes easy. Pay yourself first. It's that simple but it makes the difference between becoming financially independent and just scraping by.

Time is Money

Money grows with time. The earlier you start saving, the more money you will have. The example below shows this principle at work.

Name	Yearly savings	Age started saving	Age stopped saving	Years saved	Total investment	Interest rate	Savings at age 65
Connor	2,000	22	31	9 years	$18,000	9%	$579,471
Jasmine	2,000	31	65	35 years	$70,000	9%	$470,249

Connor has only saved for nine years. Jasmine has saved for 35 years but her savings will never match Connor's. The reason for this can be explained in two words, compound interest. When you invest your money, it earns interest. Your interest then earns interest. This is how your money grows. This is how your money works so you don't have to.

Interest Explained

There are two types of interest: simple interest and compound interest. Simple interest is the interest you earn based on the principle amount. With compound interest, interest is earned on the principle plus the interest earned.

To calculate simple interest:

Principal × % interest rate × # of years = amount earned

Example: You have $100 in your account at an interest rate of 6%.

$100 × 0.06 × 1 = $6

Every year you will earn $6. At the end of two years you would have $112.

To calculate compound interest:

(Principal + earned interest) × % interest rate × # of years = amount earned

Let's take that same savings account from the first example but let's change it to compound interest.

$100 × 0.06 × 1 = $6

Now, let's look at what happens in the second year.

($100 + $6) × 0.06 × 1 = $6.36

In the second year you would have $112.36 in your savings account instead of $100. That may not sound like much but this next example clearly illustrates the benefits of compound interest.

Years Invested	Principal	Simple Interest (10%)	Compound Interest (10%)
1	1, 000	$1,100	$1,100.00
2		$1,200	$1,210.00
3		$1,300	$1,331.00
4		$1,400	$1,464.10
5		$1,500	$1,610.51
6		$1,600	$1,771.56
7		$1,700	$1,948.72
8		$1,800	$2,143.60
9		$1,900	$2,357.96
10		$2,000	$2,593.76
11		$2,100	$2,853.14
12		$2,200	$3,138.45
13		$2,300	$3452.30
14		$2,400	$3,797.53
15		$2,500	$4,177.28
16		$2,600	$4,595.00
17		$2,700	$5,054.50
18		$2,800	$5,559.95
19		$2,900	$6,115.95
20		$3,000	$6,727.54

The amount earned with compound interest is more than double the amount earned with simple interest.

Pay Yourself First

I can't stress the importance of this rule. You **must** pay yourself a minimum of 10 percent of your earnings. Never pay yourself less than 10 percent. Even if you feel overwhelmed by bills, you still pay yourself this 10 percent. Once you pay yourself this 10 percent, that money becomes off limits. It will be used in investing and investing only.

Most of us adjust our lifestyle to the amount we make without even realizing it. We are given a raise and somehow we still don't have savings at the end of the month. Why does this happen? If you don't have a plan for savings it doesn't matter how much money you earn, you will never be financially independent. This is why we hear so many stories of people who win the lottery, going bankrupt. If you don't manage your money wisely it's easy for your spending to exceed your income. Always paying yourself first is a huge first step in fixing this problem. The money you put aside paves your path to financial freedom.

I encourage you to use the pay-yourself-first rule in all aspects of your life. If you receive money for a birthday, put 10 percent of it in savings. If you earn a bonus, you will set 10 percent of that bonus aside. Even if you win your hockey pool, you guessed it, pay yourself 10 percent of the winnings.

I have another important rule to help you manage the 10 percent you set aside for yourself. Put this money into an account that you will never touch.

Consider this money off limits. If you follow this rule, you will watch your savings grow and earn even more money for you.

Six Categories of Savings

The biggest reason for failing to manage our money lies in not understanding how to. Many of us are not taught how to properly deal with our money. But, money management is the axis on which our economic world spins. If you didn't learn money management as a child, it's time to start. You can't afford not to.

Goals such as going to university or buying a house become impossible if you can't create the finances needed to achieve these goals. Living paycheck to paycheck may seem to work okay until you miss one of those paychecks. Without savings you are left unprepared for emergencies. Without savings you lack the resources to reach your goals. Saving gives you the power to decide how you want to live your life. You decide what goals you will reach.

I've developed a money management system that uses six money accounts. Each of these six accounts has a different purpose. By using this system you will build your savings and achieve financial security.

Account #1: Riches (10 percent)

This is the account where the money from the pay-yourself-first rule goes. This is the account you never touch, allowing it to grow for your future. This money is regularly invested so it can earn interest, creating more wealth for you.

Account #2: Expenses (50 percent)

This account covers your living expenses. It includes your rent or mortgage payment, bills, clothing, car expenses, and groceries. You may have to put more than 50 percent in this category to start but try to aim for 50 percent. This will become easier as you pay closer attention to your finances.

Account #3: Savings (10 percent)

This account is where savings that you will spend later will go. You use this to pay for items you really need or want such as a new car, a vacation, or a new television. It can also be used for emergencies.

Account #4: Education (10 percent)

This is used for university, technical school, or life-long learning opportunities. Even if you have completed your education, use this money to pay for seminars or conferences in areas that are of interest to you. Maybe you can even use this money to attend conferences on money management to help increase your wealth.

Account #5: Fun (10 percent)

This account is for whatever you like whether it's going to the movies, theater, or out for supper. Go wild with this money. This is your reward for properly dividing your other funds.

Account #6: Giving (5-10 percent)

This account is for charitable donations. I truly believe that whatever you give, you will receive back.

Identify causes that are important to you and support them. Our world becomes a much richer place to live when we help others.

Practice, Practice, Practice
Like anything in life, you will not be perfect at money management from day one. It requires time and practice. Practice money management until it becomes a habit. Help your children practice their money management so they are prepared for their futures.

Money management will transform the way you view your income. Rather than always being strapped for cash, you will see your savings grow. You will start to create more income for yourself when you begin to invest the money you have paid yourself first.

What You Should Have Learned From This Chapter

❖ Pay yourself first, no matter what!

❖ Invest 10 percent of your income and let your savings work for you.

❖ Make money management a habit.

❖ Use the six accounts to work towards your financial goals.

❖ Teach your children about financial planning.

10

PUT YOUR MONEY TO WORK

Money is the seed of money, and the first guinea is sometimes more difficult to acquire than the second million.

—Jean Jacques Rousseau

Taking the Next Step

By setting goals, embracing money management, and visualizing your success you are taking the steps required to become financially independent.

Instead of only dreaming about what you want, or blaming your lack of wealth on a low paying job, you are taking the necessary steps to ensure your future success.

I hear a lot of people say, "I don't want to be rich. I just want to be comfortable." Well guess what! All of these steps are designed to make you financially comfortable. They are designed to ensure that money is not a stress in your life. Seventy percent of people worry about money every day. Don't you want to stop worrying?

Investing your Money

Now that you are on your way to mastering money management, you need to know where you should invest your money in order to earn the best rate of return. In general, there are four categories where people invest their money. These are not the only types of investments. There are countless ways you can invest your money but these will give you a good starting point.

Bonds: A bond is an amount you lend to a government or corporation. The terms of repayment are outlined so you earn money on the amount you have lent.

A buyer purchases bonds at a fixed interest rate for a period of time. When that period of time has expired, the bond is said to have matured. The buyer may then redeem the bond for the full value. If you choose to invest in a bond you will not have easy access to this money.

Bonds can be corporate (sold by private companies), municipal (issued by nonfederal governments), and federal (issued by the federal government) which is the lowest risk bond.

Mutual Funds: These are professionally run portfolios comprised of stocks, bonds, and other investments.

When you purchase a mutual fund you buy shares in a fund which purchases stocks, bonds, or other investments. Mutual funds allow a small investor to take advantage of professional account management that is normally only available to larger investors.

Types of mutual funds include balanced funds, global bond funds, growth funds, income funds, and regional stock funds. There are many other types as well.

Stocks: Owning a stock means you own a part of a company. Stockholders are entitled to a share of a company's profits and may vote on how the company is run.

The company's profits are divided among stockholders in the form of dividends which are usually paid quarterly. Investors will also benefit if the price of a company's shares increases. Shares are bought and sold on stock exchanges like the Toronto Stock Exchange and the New York Stock Exchange.

Stocks allow their investors easy access to their money.

Real Estate: This is property that is purchased and held as a long-term investment or sold for a short-term gain. The goal with real estate is to buy low and sell high.

Real estate doesn't transfer to cash quickly.

I started my road to riches by building my first house as a teenager. I realized I was good at this, so I built more houses and sold them. I used these profits to build a real estate company which I sold to buy a ski resort. With each step I was working towards becoming financially independent.

If you want to build wealth, you need to build assets. An asset is something that gives money back to you, without you having to work. Real estate tends to increase in value over time and you can also earn money by renting the property to someone else. Stocks may also increase in value over time and you can also earn money from dividends. Once you build up one asset, use it to build up more. This will give you several sources of income.

It's important to have a plan in place for what you will do with your savings once they reach a substantial size, around $1,000. What do you want to invest in? Where do you think you can make the most money?

I made much of my money in real estate. I enjoy the real estate market so it's been a good fit for me. Some of you might enjoy playing the stock market. Some might want others to manage their money so mutual funds would be a good idea. Do what you enjoy when investing and building your riches.

With real estate, I invest money in an area where there will be future land growth. This means where I believe my land will go up in value. In a town that is growing on the west side, I purchase real estate on the west side. I try to buy land that is currently a little out of the way but will cease to be out of the way once the town grows. I then sell the land once it's reached top dollar or I develop it and rent out the buildings.

I do a lot of research before any of my real estate deals. Regardless of where you want to invest, you will need to research it first. Have fun with this. You're investing in your future.

What You Should Have Learned From This Chapter

❖ When considering how you will invest; bonds, stocks, mutual funds, and real estate are good options to look into.

❖ Have a plan to invest your savings even if you haven't earned them yet.

❖ Research your investments.

❖ Investments make your money work for you 24 hours a day, 365 days a year.

YOU'RE RICHER THAN YOU THINK

There are people who have money and people who are rich.

—Coco Chanel

The decision to take control of your finances and work towards wealth may feel like it's a small step on a thousand mile journey. This is a good thing. It's when all of your decisions seem easy that you should worry. By deciding to build your wealth and teach your children how to do the same, you've made the decision to do something really special. Many of us think of wealth only as a concept, not something we could ever possibly attain. Some people are born with a gift to make money, we think, some people are lucky enough to be born into wealth.

This couldn't be further from the truth. Stop thinking of wealth as a concept and start thinking about the kind of wealth you want to create.

Hone Your Talent

What do you love to do? When I started out in the working world, I would have run into a whole heap of trouble if I had decided to pursue medicine or law. I wasn't born with a natural talent or interest in either of those fields. We think of doctors and lawyers as people who make a lot of money. But in order to be successful in either, you need to be incredibly passionate about your work. This is true of whatever field you may decide to pursue.

When deciding what you want to do for a living, don't just choose a profession that will make you a lot of money. Instead, focus on what you enjoy doing. If you don't love what you do, you won't be willing to overcome the obstacles that will be placed in your path. I focused on construction because I enjoyed construction. I was able to turn this passion into a very profitable business. My work in construction allowed me to develop a passion for real estate. By focusing on what I was interested in rather than where I would make the most money I have achieved things that, at one time, I would have told you were impossible.

I want you to answer the following questions:

What are my hobbies?

Of those hobbies, which two am I most passionate about?

What do others say I am good at?

What skill have I been putting off that I would like to develop?

If I didn't have to go to work tomorrow, what would I do?

Examine your answers. Are there any common themes that come up? Although some of us have trouble admitting it, we have been born with many natural talents. Some are great leaders. Some are born with the minds of artists. And some are born with an eye for business. All of these are personal assets. We can use these gifts to create wealth for ourselves. I'm not saying you need to quit your job and focus on your love of gardening. But by focusing on our skills, we open new opportunities for ourselves. Don't ignore your gifts. You never know where they may lead you.

Pay it Forward

When we feel it is impossible to improve our lives, we seize up. We keep everything for ourselves because there may be a day when we have nothing. I mentioned how most of us view wealth only as a concept. We need to stop looking at wealth in that way. When we look closely at our lives, we can readily identify areas in which we are wealthy. Identify the areas of your life in which you are rich and pay those areas forward. Believe in yourself and offer your gifts to others, whether it's through charitable donations, volunteer work, or simply offering your skills to a friend in need. Whatever you give out is multiplied when it is returned to you.

Paying it forward is important because in offering, you are recognizing you have something to offer. By saying you can help, you are proclaiming your talents and skills. By giving, you are recognizing that you have enough and can help others. I have talked about our world becoming a richer place when we give back.

When we give, we become richer people in more areas than just financial.

Whatever You Give, You Get

I've talked about how important it is to believe you will be wealthy in order to become wealthy. The energy we send out always comes back to us—always. If you think you will never succeed, everything that surrounds you communicates that idea, even if you aren't saying it in words. It's impossible to get ahead if you walk around silently proclaiming, "Stay away from me! I'm not going anywhere and I'll bring you down with me."

But, if you truly believe you will succeed, and keep that idea in the back of your mind at all times, you can't help but succeed. Words and thoughts are powerful things. By saying you know you can, you can. By focusing on success rather than failure, guess what? You achieve success. It's not necessarily the person with the greatest skill who wins; it's the person who believes in herself the most. Think about it, who would you rather surround yourself with, those who go around thinking the worst or those who truly believe they will succeed?

Negative energy attracts negative energy. Positive energy attracts positive energy. I think this is pretty logical. We want to be around people that build us up rather than tear us down. What kind of energy are you sending out? Is it working for you? If not, adjust your thinking. Choose to believe in yourself. Choose to be positive. I guarantee you will receive much in return.

What You Should Have Learned From This Chapter

- ❖ Your talents are personal assets.

- ❖ Focus on your talents rather than an area in which you think you will be the most profitable.

- ❖ By giving to others, you receive much in return.

- ❖ Negative thoughts attract negative results.

- ❖ If you think you will succeed, you will.

12

PUT YOUR MONEY TO WORK

*"If you work for money, you give the power to your employer.
If money works for you, you keep and control the power."*

—Robert T. Kiyosaki

So far, we've discussed a lot of concepts and ideas about getting your attitude and your money to work for you so you can achieve a better life. It's time now to begin to put those concepts and ideas into practice. The remainder of this book consists of activities that will help families put the skills they need into place so they can achieve the greatest possible success. But first, a word to parents:

The learning process can bring out both the best and the worst in parents and children. That's because you know each other so well. Many parents tell me that their children learn more readily when they are taught by people who are not family members. Teenagers in particular can be frustrating for a parent to work with, especially if the teen doesn't want to do the work.

Besides that, people learn in different ways: visual learners tend to think in pictures and like to be presented with diagrams and charts that illustrate what is being taught. Auditory learners pick up ideas and information by listening. Kinesthetic (or tactile) learners are doers; they're not really good at reading directions before they begin, preferring to plunge right into an activity and learn as they go along.

Teaching visual and auditory learners is generally easier than teaching kinesthetic/tactile learners because they can read or listen to the directions before you begin. For kinesthetic/tactile learners, role playing and games tend to work best. Of course everybody has a bit of each learning style in their make-up, but it's fairly easy to figure out which style is dominant in yourself and others. Once you know that, you can decide how to teach them.

I have always thought that playing board games like Monopoly, Risk, or Pictionary are great ways to learn life skills. They're fun and they teach the exact skills your kids will eventually need to succeed in whatever they choose to do. So I urge you to play these types of games with your kids and encourage them to apply the skills they learn in real life situations when appropriate.

To get the most out of this book, get the whole family—especially you as parents—involved in the activities that follow. They've been designed to apply the theoretical concepts we've been discussing to real life situations. Schedule a family meeting twice a month to go through them and make the activities fun—perhaps by adding an element of competition.

Now I have to warn you—most people won't bother to do these activities. That will be their loss. Remember, you only have so much time with your kids as they grow up. Once they've flown the nest, the opportunity to teach them these skills will likely be gone forever. So give these money management skills the same priority you give activities like soccer or hockey.

It isn't difficult, so just do it!

WORKBOOK

ACTIVITY 1

Adopting an "I Can" Attitude

This is a great activity to identify the self-limiting and empowering beliefs the members of your family have at present. It works best if you do the activity together rather than separately. Make sure each family member has a copy of the questions and that each of you answers them without consulting the others.

Once you've prepared your lists to the best of your ability, share them with the others and help each other refine your lists.

You'll need more room than is provided here so make sure each family member has a notebook to keep a record of each activity so you can refer back to it later.

This is a three-part activity so you may wish to spread it out over three evenings, doing one part at a time.

PART I:

1. List what you believe are your personal limitations. For example…

   I can't _____

   I never _____

   I will never _____

   I do not like _____

2. List what you believe are your family's limitations. For example…

   We don't ever _____

   We never go _____

   We can't have _____

   We don't believe that _____

3. Take each of the statements you made in (1.) and turn them from negative statements to positive statements—statements which start with the words "I can." If you find you need help doing this, reread **Chapter 3: Keep Your Eyes on the Prize.**
4. Take each of the statements you made in (2.) and turn them into positive statements as well—statements that begin with the words "We can."

PART II:

1. Draw up a list of your positive beliefs about yourself. For example...
   I am _____
   I have _____
   I enjoy _____
   I am able to _____
2. Draw up a list of your positive beliefs about your family. For example...
   We are very good at _____
   We enjoy _____
   We love _____
   We believe that _____
   We have always had _____

PART III:

1. Write four unique positive statements about yourself. They should all start with the words "I Can" or "I Am." Post these around the house where you will see them, and put the best one in your wallet so you can read it during the day. Here are some examples...

   "I can save money because now I know how to use money management."

"I can improve my school marks because I am concentrating better than ever before."

2. Write four different positive statements about your family—statements that are also unique and that begin with the words "Our family can." Tack these statements up on the family bulletin board or stick them on the refrigerator where everybody can see them. Here are some examples…

"Our family can establish goals and together we will achieve them."

"Our family members can discuss money issues seriously."

ACTIVITY 2

A Night at the Movies
Spend an evening together as a family watching one of your favorite movies. Don't have a favorite? Here are some options.

For kids under age 8
The Sound of Music, The Lion King, Shrek

For kids aged 9 and 10
The Princess Bride, E.T. the Extra-Terrestrial

For preteens and teenagers
Hoosiers, Field of Dreams, Mr. Holland's Opus

Movie nights are fun family events. Choose films that incorporate family values and beliefs. Sports-themed movies are particularly good because they usually tell stories about an underdog who overcomes adversity to become a success.

After watching the movie, talk about the challenges faced by the characters and how they overcame failures and obstacles to achieve success in the end.

Here are some questions to help you lead the discussion:

1. What were the attitudes of some of the main characters at the start of the story?
2. How did these attitudes change as the story progressed?
3. What was it that persuaded the main characters to pursue their goals and dreams?
4. How did the attitude of the main character affect the attitudes of other characters in the film?
5. How did the coach/teacher/parent encourage the other characters/
6. What were some of the things that the coach/teacher/parent tried that didn't work? Why didn't they work?
7. How did some of the characters react to failure? What did they do about it?
8. How did things turn out in the end?
9. What were some of the important things the characters did or said that led to the results?
10. Which character was the most inspiring? Why?

(ACTIVITY 3)

Evaluate Your Inner Wealth

I suggest your family take this survey together although you can do it on your own if you wish. My suggestion is to go through the survey questions one by one, with each family member contributing his or her answer. Or you can answer the questions in writing in your notebooks and discuss your answers around the table.

When setting out your personal assets, don't be self-conscious or shy. And help each other as you go through the results, adding those that come to mind as you go along. Teenagers and adults will find it easier than small children to fill in the first five categories so I've included a special section for small children and preteens so the entire family can be included in this activity.

The instructions are simple: make a list of your assets in each category listed. Remember, these are not physical assets like strength or athletic ability. They are intangibles like honesty, helpfulness, artistic abilities, etc.

1. Personal Characteristics (i.e. honesty, integrity, perseverance)
2. Personal Talents (i.e. writing ability, good with numbers, artistic gifts)
3. Personal Expertise: What are you knowledgeable about? (accounting, computers, construction)
4. What specific leadership qualities and experience do you have?
5. What specific organizational skills do you have?

Children's Survey (Ask your parents for help if you need it)

1. List your good qualities (include things like 'honest', 'helpful' and others)
2. List things you like to do or are good at (like reading, writing, dancing or playing a musical instrument)
3. List things you have learned about and things you would like to learn about.
4. List activities you are in where you are a leader or are learning to be a leader.
5. List activities at home or at school where you organize things.

ACTIVITY 4

The Law of Attraction

This activity is intended to help your family understand the Law of Attraction. It's another Movie Night.

Rent the movie *The Secret* and watch it together as a family. When the movie is over, discuss the Law of Attraction and share what each of you learned from the film. Here are some questions to guide your discussion:

1. What is the Law of Attraction and how does it work?
2. Have there been times when you concentrated on what you didn't want rather than what you did want? Talk about these.
3. Has the Law of Attraction ever resulting in you getting something you wanted? Talk about what you

did to activate the Law of Attraction and what happened when you did.

4. How can you use the Law of Attraction to get something you want?
5. As a family, what would you most like to attract using the Law of Attraction?

What Do You Want?

This is the most important question you and your family will have to answer. And you have to be very specific.

As a family, create a list of the things you want. It doesn't have to be a long list (although it can be) and it's not a shopping list of the things you'd like to have. No, this is a list of the important things you want. So sit down as a family and carefully decide what will go on it. Make sure each family member knows what's on the list and understands why you want it.

Then begin to imaging that you already have one of the short term items. Think about it, feel it, taste it, hear it and most of all, enjoy having it.

Concentrate on one thing at a time. The Law of Attraction doesn't work as well when you send out several thoughts about different things. Concentrating on one thing at a time focuses your energy more powerfully on the thing you are attracting.

Discuss what happens, then start focusing on the next item.

Keep a Success Journal

Every time you notice the Law of Attraction working for you, make a note of it. Do this even for the small things.

Journaling creates a record of how the Law of Attraction can work in your life and helps you learn to use the Law of Attraction in different ways. As you notice it working, you will use it more successfully and your ability to focus will continue to increase.

Develop an Attitude of Gratitude

Take some time every day to be grateful for what you have. It may be your home, your health, your family, loved ones, possessions—any of the myriad of things that are part of your life. If you take the time to experience gratitude, the universe will help you receive even more so you will be doubly grateful.

Keep a journal to write down the things you are grateful for. An entry might be "I am grateful for the new job offer I received today" or "I am happy that I found the perfect suit of clothes to wear to my daughter's wedding."

ACTIVITY 5

Discovering the Riches Around you

This is a simple Internet research project.

Have each member of your family select a business who is wealthy and successful—Bill Gates, Donald Trump, Wally 'Famous' Amos and Warren Buffet, for example—and learn about that person using the Internet. Find out as much as you can about their childhood, businesses, how they made their fortunes and what they are doing today.

You'll find that some people inherited wealth; others came up from very humble beginnings. All of them had to learn to manage their money at some point and many suffered failures before they became successful.

Learn their stories and share the information over dinner. Discuss the lessons you learn from studying their success stories.

Are the lessons in this book similar to the experiences of these successful business people?

ACTIVITY 6

Games That Each Money Management
Monopoly is a game that teaches everyone who plays it how to make and manage money. Add a rule that 10 percent of everything a player earns must be placed in a savings account or invested in properties, railroads or utilities. It will teach your children what can happen when they save and invest regularly.

Two other excellent games are *Cashflow* and *Cashflow for Kids* created by Robert Kiyosaki. They demonstrate how proper money management can get you out of the rat race. I know 40-year-olds who still play *Cashflow* regularly and swear it teaches them something new every time.

Try it and see if it helps you manage money in real life.

ACTIVITY 7

Setting Your Personal Goals
This activity helps you set the personal goals that are essential to your success. As part of this activity, each family member will set his or her personal goals.

After each person has completed a Goal Sheet, have a show-and-tell session at which family member tells the others about his or her goals.

You only require one or two goals at the beginning. Make one a financial goal. After you set and achieve a few goals, you may want to set more. Use the personal goal sheet template as a format. Complete new goals sheets every three months.

After three, six and 12 months, have a family discussion about the goals you have set and achieved. Remember to celebrate your successes!

Your Personal Goal Statements

The best goal statements are: formatted in the *Pre*sent tense; *E*motional; *R*ealistic; *M*easurable; *A*ction-based. The acronym is **PERMA**, which stands for **permanent**.

Your Personal Goals

Goal #1　　Completion Date _____

Goal #2　　Completion Date _____

Remember, setting and achieving goals is a proven way to achieve wealth.

ACTIVITY 8

Family Goals

Once you have established your personal goals, you should get together and set family goals as well. These, of course, are goals your family will achieve by working together. These types of goals are things you will want to do together. They could include going on a vacation, volunteering to work at the local food bank, learning to play musical instruments—things like that.

Once you have set your goals and decided how they will be reached, post them on the family bulletin board or the refrigerator where everybody can see them and encourage other members of the family to work on achieving them. Complete a new Family Goal Statement every three months.

Your Family Goal Statements

Like personal goal statements, the best family goal statements are: formatted in the *P*resent tense; *E*motional; *R*ealistic; *M*easurable; *A*ction-based. The acronym is **PERMA**, which stands for **permanent.**

> **Your Family Goals**
> Goal #1   **Completion Date** _____
>
> Goal #2   **Completion Date** _____

As with personal goals, setting and achieving family goals is a proven way to achieve wealth.

(ACTIVITY 9)

Overcoming Barriers to Goal Achievement

You are always going to encounter barriers as you go about achieving your goals. The first thing you have to do is identify them. Then you have to remove them or overcome them. This exercise helps you identify obstacles and come up with ways to overcome them as you travel your road to success.

First of all, answer these questions…

1. What are the barriers that are keeping me from being more successful?
2. What are the barriers that are keeping our family from being more successful?
3. What creative ways can I use to eliminate these barriers? *(Make a list of ideas without judging whether they are good or bad. Once your list is complete, select the best two or three ideas and try them first.)*
4. How will eliminating these obstacles help me (our family) become more successful?

ACTIVITY 10

A Family Competition
Make a simple chart for the family bulletin board or the refrigerator. The chart should have one column for each member of the family, with each person's name at the top of one column.

Every time you hear a family member begin a statement with a negative word (*don't, not, no, never,* etc.) put a checkmark in the column under that person's name. See who has the fewest checkmarks at the end of the week.

This should be done in a spirit of pure fun. Kids especially like to catch their parents.

ACTIVITY 11

Word Pictures
For each of the terms below, ask each family member to draw a picture that demonstrates its meaning. This

is a great way to help younger children learn to associate words and pictures.

Words to draw: Dream
                Budget
                Money
                Invest
                Savings Account
                The Law of Attraction
                Money Management
                Vibrations (or Vibes)

Encourage them to go back through the book or look at the glossary of terms in The Language of Money section beginning on Page XX to find other words that can be included in this activity.

ACTIVITY 12

Field Trips

Visits to businesses are among the best ways to teach children about the real world and how successful businesses operate. If possible, involve your children in planning the trip by letting them choose where they want to go. Some high schools have mentorship programs which team business people with students who want to learn what goes on in the real world of business.

One of your first field trips should be to a **bank**. If your child does not already have a savings account, this would be a good time to open one. People your kids should meet include a teller, a customer assistant and loan officer. They can tell your child what they do and how the bank works by telling them about things like chequing and savings accounts, how to make deposits and withdrawals and what the interest rates are for saving and borrowing money.

Encourage your child to ask questions about the various kinds of loans the bank can make and also about the difference between credit and debit cards.

Of course you should touch base with the bank manager to arrange your visit at a time when it is not busy and the staff will have time to visit with you. I think you'll find most bank managers will be very happy to accommodate you.

A visit to a local **grocery store** can be an opportunity to teach the kids about getting good value for their money. Show them how to compare products and prices to get quality food at reasonable cost. Learning to buy quality food without paying premium prices helps them recognize the relationship between quality and pricing. One of the most important lessons to be learned from a trip to a grocery store is to compare unit prices. A one kilogram container may cost less per 100 grams than a 500-gram container of the same product, for example. And sometimes it is better to purchase the more expensive brand if the quality is better. You can explain this reasoning to your children as you go through your weekly grocery list.

When you go through the checkout line, have your children watch the cashier scan the items, then let them complete the transaction. This helps them to get to know the cost of household necessities before they leave home.

Make arrangements to go to a **real estate office** and meet an agent. Discuss the process of buying a home—including mortgages, fees, real estate agent commissions and property title searches. It doesn't have to be detailed, just enough for the kids to understand the basics of the process they'll go through when they eventually buy their own home.

If you are in the market for a new car, a trip to an **automobile dealership** would be very interesting, particularly to a teenager who is approaching driving age. Take your child along when you look at new and used cars. Talk to a credit officer about the way cars are financed and the importance of establishing and maintaining good credit.

If you use and **investment or brokerage firm**, make arrangements to spend some time with a broker who can tell you about stocks and bonds, types of investments and rates of return. You don't have to go into great detail but you'll wan tot touch on how to decide what types of investments to make and how you set up an account. If you have a teenager who has been earning some money, he or she might even want to open a small account.

ACTIVITY 13

Celebrating Family Successes

Overcoming obstacles and removing barriers at school or at work is something the whole family should celebrate. Your kids in particular, should be rewarded when they apply the lessons learned in this book.

Create some rewards that family members can earn—things like a free ticket to a movie, a pass that allows your son to get out of making his bed for a day, a meal for Mon cooked by Dad and the kids.

A Family Outing
Allow your teenagers to plan a weekend trip or family outing to somewhere the entire family wants to go. Let the kids do all the planning and finance it from money the family has earned together.

Play "Risk"
"Risk: is a board game that involves evaluating risk, making decisions and working with others. As the title suggests, it also involves deciding which risks you will take. It's a great way to learn to evaluate risks.

ACTIVITY 14

Using Your Mental Faculties
Think of your mental faculties as 'muscles' that you can use to help you build prosperity. Here are some activities to help you develop these mental muscles. There are a lot of them outlined here but I suggest you limit yourself to one per evening.

To recap what we learned earlier, your six mental faculties are **Perception, Reasoning, Memory, Intuition, Will** and **Imagination**. Here are some activity suggestions for each of them:

Perception deals with how you look at yourself and the world around you. It can be a difficult concept for younger children to grasp, so be sure you discuss it with them first. Then, together, make a list of words that describe each member of the family. You don't need to go into great detail—two or three words per person will suffice—but the words should be positive.

Print each word on a separate post-it note and place the notes in a bowl. Mix them up and then take turns pulling out notes one by one. Read the word and have family members guess who it describes.

This game will help you discover how your children perceive themselves and you but remember, it's just a game so don't be too concerned about the kinds of words your young children come up with.

If your children are all over 10 years of age, discuss what perception means and then get each family member to come up with the three or four words that best describes him or her. Share your words with each other. This is a great activity to do over dinner. Just remember to keep it light and fun.

Reasoning is how we figure things out. Board games like Clue, Boggle or Pictionary are great ways to develop your reasoning ability. Remember to choose a game that that's appropriate for your children's age level. I'd also advise you to stay away from video or computer games. One of the main objects of this activity is to stimulate interaction between parents and kids. Board games do that; video games don't.

After the game, talk about the reasoning and strategies you each used to help you think things through. And as always, keep it fun!

Memory is something everyone has to exercise throughout their lifetime. It is literally true that 'if you don't use it, you lose it!'

One of the best memory games is Concentration. You can buy the board game or—and this is much easier and cheaper—use a deck of playing cards. Place the cards face down on the table and turn over two at a time. If the cards match, you keep the pair and take another turn. When all the cards are gone, the person with the most pairs is the winner.

Another way to exercise the memory is to discuss your favorite movie, recalling the plot, main characters and the actors. In fact any discussion that requires the use of the memory faculty is a good activity. Just remember to keep it short and make it fun.

Intuition is a difficult concept for anyone to fully understand but it's especially hard for younger children. You will want to spend some time one-on-one with your little ones explaining how it is sometimes possible to 'just know' something. Tell them it's OK if they don't understand intuition right now. They'll learn more about it when they're a bit older.

While they're still young, it is enough to tell them a story about a character that has good intuition. You can find lots of them on the Internet by searching for *stories about intuition*. You might also want to watch one of the early Harry Potter movies and discuss how Harry and his friends use their intuition.

When discussing intuition with older children, make certain you tell them that it's okay to trust your feelings. For example, if they are in a situation where they feel threatened by something, their intuition may be making them anxious and they need to pay attention to it. Children—particularly teenagers—should not be discouraged from paying attention to their feelings.

Will is something that's familiar to most parents. At one time or another, most children exhibit strong-willed tendencies. Sadly children are usually punished for this behavior because it is usually expressed in a negative way. However as parents, we should also try to develop the positive aspects of this mental faculty so children can use it to accomplish their goals.

Why do we need to develop this mental faculty? It is because "the most valuable education is that which trains us to do what should be done, when it should be done, whether we feel like it or not," according to author Frank Tibolt.

The way to develop willpower is to take on a challenge that requires persistence and willpower to achieve. It should be something that's fun, like a service project. If you have both teens and younger children, you may wish to do different projects with each. Once again, it should be something fun like participating in a walkathon or a bike ride. Include the children in making the decision about what you with to do. If they are involved in making the decision, they will embrace the activity more whole-heartedly.

Remember the point of doing something together is to teach how willpower and persistence can accomplish goals. So choose something that will successfully reward the effort you put into it.

There is a web site called *HelpOthers.org* that has a page of Kindness Ideas—things you can do for others without being asked. It will provide you with additional suggestions.

Imagination is the process of generating ideas. So by thinking of things you want to do, you are using your imagination. The options here are limitless.

Younger children can draw pictures of what they want to be when they grow up.

As a family, you can go on a safari from the comfort of the living-room sofa! Choose someone to be the pilot of the plane, fasten your seat belts, and fly away to distant lands. Anyone suffering from restlessness during the journey can take on the role of steward and serve imaginary drinks and peanuts (or even real ones!) Keep an eye out for amazing sights as you fly—the tiny rivers and mountains below, beautiful clouds and, of course, the wild animals. When you do spot something, it's time to perform your best impression of a gorilla, parrot, snake, giraffe, crocodile, etc.

On a sunny summer day, take the entire family to a park and have everyone lie down and gaze up into the sky. While you're looking up, discuss:

- Where would you fly to?
- How high would you fly if there were no limits?
- What would it look like and feel like to be up in the air?
- Who would you want to fly with? It could be anyone?

As often as you can, take time to be with your kids and talk about their dreams. Encourage them and find out what they want out of life—both personally and professionally.

Reading List
I have read literally hundreds of books about creating wealth, health and happiness during my lifetime. The books I've listed here are the best I have come across,

written by experts in their fields. You will recognize many of their names.

Some of these books have withstood the test of time and their message is as valid today as it was when they were written decades ago. Others are more recent but still convey the kind of thinking that has always been useful to me.

The list is short, but by the time you get through it you'll have learned about many other sources that you'll be able refer to for the rest of your life.

Books
Working With The Law—by Raymond Holliwell
>   A timeless classic about how to use the Law of Attraction

The One-Minute Millionaire—by Mark Victor Hansen and Robert Allen
>   A mix of self-help and money talk by two of today's best-selling authors

The Science of Getting Rich—by Wallace D. Wattles
>   Published in 1910, you can download it free. Google the title

Think and Grow Rich—by Napoleon Hill
>   Published in 1937, it remains a perennial best-seller after 70 years

Multimedia
The Secret—the classic movie about the Law of Attraction
The Strangest Secret—by Earl Nightingale
>   One of the most powerful and influential audio messages ever recorded

Just do it!